Contrasts

Comparative Essays
on Italian-Canadian Writing

Picas Series 3

Contrasts

Comparative Essays
on Italian-Canadian Writing

Edited by
Joseph Pivato

Guernica

Montreal, 1991

Copyright © 1985, 1991 by Joseph Pivato
and Guernica Editions.
First published in this format 1991.

All rights reserved.
Printed in Canada.
Typeset by Atelier LHR

Guernica Editions, P.O. Box 633, Station N.D.G.,
Montréal (Québec), Canada H4A 3R1

Dépôt légal — 3e trimestre 1991
Bibliothèque nationale du Québec &
National Library of Canada

Canadian Cataloguing in Publication Data
Main entry under title:
Contrasts: comparative essays on Italian-Canadian writing

(Picas series; 3)
Bibliography: p. 231
ISBN 9-920717-35-7

1. Canadian literature — Italian-Canadian authors — History and
criticism. 2. Canadian literature (Italian) — History and criticism.
I. Pivato, Joseph II. Series.

PS8089.5.I8C65 1989   C810'.9;851   C88-090332-5
PR9188.2.I82C65 1989

To the Memory of
Dino Minni
Robert Billings
Gianni Grohovaz
Elena Maccaferri Randaccio
Ottorino Bressan
and
Robert Harney

Table of Contents

Introduction: Why Comparative Essays?,
Joseph Pivato 9

*Ethnic Writing and Comparative
Canadian Literature*, Joseph Pivato 15

*Tasks of the Canadian Novelist Writing
on Immigrant Themes*, F.G. Paci 35

The Short Story as an Ethnic Genre, C.D. Minni . . 61

Black Madonna: *A Search for the Great Mother*,
Roberta Sciff-Zamaro 77

*Death Between Two Cultures:
Italian-Canadian Poetry*, Alexandre L. Amprimoz
and Sante A. Viselli 101

*Contemporary Influences on the Poetry
of Mary di Michele*, Robert Billings 121

The Italian Writer and Language, Fulvio Caccia . . . 153

*A Literature of Exile:
Italian Language Writing in Canada*,
Joseph Pivato 169

The Italian Writers of Quebec:
Language, Culture and Politics, Filippo Salvatore 189

The Road Between: Essentialism.
For an Italian Culture in Quebec and Canada,
Antonio D'Alfonso 207

Selected Bibliography 231

Notes on Contributors 249

Index of Writers 251

Acknowledgements 257

JOSEPH PIVATO

Introduction
Why Comparative Essays?

Looking into my sister's eyes
I see Italia behind my shoulders.

Mary di Michele

This collection of essays is paradoxical. On the one hand it examines works from a minority literature, in fact, a minority literature within a minority literature. On the other hand it studies these literary works in the context of world literature rather than just a national literature. Despite the apparent contradiction there are several reasons for reading Italian-Canadian writing in this comparative manner. Probably more than other ethnic literatures Italian-Canadian writing does not fit easily into one cultural tradition. It exists in English, French and Italian and is influenced by all three literary traditions. A comparative approach is the best way of dealing with this trilingual phenomenon. The authors are consciously writing in an international context that includes an awareness of literature from both Europe and the New World, and in particular works in English, French, Italian and Spanish. The works often deal with the experience of immigration in Canada. Immigration, however, rather than being a narrow occurrence is one with international associations. In the modern world dislocation is a universal human experience and thus Canadian immigrant writing speaks to a wide spectrum of mankind. For some readers the writing of Italian-Canadian authors, especially those working in Italian, is an example of Italian literature in exile, an expatriate literature, that both belongs to, and does not belong to the 600 year-old Italian literary tradition. Comparative Literature involves the study of works in the broad contexts of literary relations, influences, genres, movements and traditions. It often deals with literary works in more than one language. It would seem therefore, that the comparative approach is the most fruitful one in reading ethnic writing. For a number of years Comparative Canadian Literature has tried to look at Canadian writing from an international perspective. Immigrant writing transcends the parochial, the provincial and national boundaries and would seem to provide an avenue to world literature and to a comparative methodology. The narrow environmentalist biases of current Canadian literary criticism are not supported by the essays in this collection.

There is an implicit rejection of the nationalistic reading of Canadian writing by the authors represented here. The essays point to a deeper truth in the art of man: it is not in the grand scale but in the little things that we find the commonality of man. The immigrant mothers in Paci's novels, the children in Minni's short stories, the confused young people in Micone's plays, the women in Ardizzi's narratives, share identifiable characteristics with people all over the world. The realistic details in the stories, the concern with language in the poetry, the search for truth in the dramatic situation are all considered in the essays assembled here.

The study of Canadian Literature has always been problematic because of the relative newness of English language writing and the lack of contact with the older francophone tradition. Attempts to draw relationships between the two have often been based more on political or historical considerations than on *rapports de fait*. In contrast ethnic writing has evolved naturally in an open cultural environment which has had few strong national traditions and few political expectations. Italian-Canadian writing has developed in a random manner with writers across the country working in isolation. It is all the more remarkable that we now find that these authors share many affinities that go beyond their Italian background or a concern with the immigrant experience. Some of these similarities will be explored in the following pages.

This book does not attempt to present a unifying theory about Canadian Literature, nor a dominant theme such as exile or survival. Each essay has an individual point of view and is comparative in varying degrees. While Frank Paci's essay looks at the Canadian novelist in the context of world literature: Robert Billings concentrates on a relatively small circle of five Canadian women poets. It may be, though, that from these modest examples of literary history we get an understanding of the process of creative writing.

Other essays take a less traditional approach to literary analysis. In her interpretation of *Black Madonna* and the myth of the Great Mother Roberta Sciff-Zamaro employs structuralist methodology. Underlying patterns are also identified in ethnic poetry by Amprimoz and Viselli. We find that the treatment of death in one form or another recurs often in the works considered here. C.D. Minni examines the genre of the short story and its relation to ethnic writing.

While the essays collected here do not demonstrate the Canadian preoccupation with our relationship to nature, they do show a strong sense of the social milieu, the family, the neighbourhood, the city. There is an awarness of history and our place in it. Fulvio Caccia's analysis of the ethnic writer in Quebec considers this sense of time and place. From the Italian-Canadian point of view Quebec has been an evolving society and we can see changes from the time Duliani published *La*

Ville sans femmes in 1945 to the plays of Micone in the 1980's. Filippo Salvatore considers the relationship between literature and the political climate in Quebec. In the last essay in this collection Antonio D'Alfonso tries to see future developments as a result of the work of Italian-Canadian writers.

In recent years several collections of Italian-Canadian writing have been published. The most significant are: *Roman Candles: An Anthology of Poems by Seventeen Italo-Canadian Poets* (1978) edited by Pier Giorgio Di Cicco, *La poesia italiana nel Quebec* (1983) edited by Tonino Caticchio, *Quêtes: Textes d'auteurs italo-québécois* (1983) edited by Fulvio Caccia and Antonio D'Alfonso, and *Italian-Canadian Voices: An Anthology of Poetry and Prose (1946-1983)* edited by Caroline Di Giovanni in 1984. In a sense this collection of essays can be viewed as a companion to these literary anthologies and to the many other individual works by Italian-Canadian authors. The selected bibliography at the end of this collection lists many of the titles by the writers discussed here.

JOSEPH PIVATO

Ethnic Writing
and Comparative Canadian
Literature

> I have written these essays... from a position that assumes, despite the fundamental differences in cultural ideologies, that Canada endures in a polysemous, polyvalent fashion.[1]

This is the approach that E.D. Blodgett takes in order to deal with the problems inherent in the comparative study of Candian writing in English and in French. These words can be used as the motto for the study of ethnic writing in North America. As the words imply, there is both a cultural and a political dimension to the interpretation of Canadian literature. There have always been pulls in different directions: centralism and regionalism, French and English, traditional and modern, native and foreign. In the past critics have tried to seek a common thread running through our literatures, but, as Philip Stratford has observed,

> Comparatists of Canadian subjects are themselves condemned to maintain a paradoxical duality. Blinded by proximity to their subject, swayed by politics and history, hamstrung by an inevitable natural, linguistic and cultural affiliation to one of two camps, they must neither unify, nor divide.[2]

Given these difficulties it is little wonder that the Comparative study of Canadian literatures, instead of thriving in our bilingual country, has remained a Cinderella both as an academic discipline and as a methodology in Canadian studies.

With his major comparative work, *Configuration: Essays on the Canadian Literatures*, E.D. Blodgett tries to resolve some of the difficulties due to a fixation with the binary approach to our culture. In order to maintain a perspective that can account for the contingent and contiguous Blodgett uses a method that looks at the inter-relationships of rhetorical figures in the works. In some of his comparative essays he deliberately focuses on the role of German writing in Canada and thus moves the national centre of gravity away from the traditional binarism of anglophone and francophone — a polarity which often gives the impression that Canada is more centripetal than it is.

Configuration is the first critical study, comparative or unilingual, that seriously considers the work of ethnic writers and their contribution to the majority literatures of Canada. While other critics have briefly considered the idea of an "ethnic voice,"[3] or the problem of "immigrant isolation,"[4] none have closely examined examples of either immigrant or foreign language writing. The work of Jewish writers in Canada has been seen as part of a North American phenomenon rather than ethnic or foreign.[5] By looking at the ethnicity of Canadian writing Blodgett has been able to bring new perspectives to the study of both anglophone and francophone literatures. *Configuration* will serve as a model, and a guide for future studies of Canadian writing from both majority and minority cultures.

The theoretical criticism and the practical analysis in Blodgett's book is all the more interesting given the rather impoverished history of the literary criticism of Canadian writing. A brief review will give some of the blaze marks that outline the narrow trail to Comparative Canadian Literature. Along the way we meet many assumptions about what constitutes a national literature in this country and thus we will be better able to see the place of ethnic writing in this rather nativist context.

The history of criticism in Canadian writing is highlighted by major literary figures from Charles G.D. Roberts in the 1890's to D.G. Jones in the 1980's. As might be expected, much comparative criticism took the form of translation between English and French writing. Charles Roberts published his transcription of Philippe Aubert de Gaspé's *Les Anciens Canadiens* in 1890. Roberts' rendition of this 1863 book included not only an English reproduction of the prose narrative but also a poetic re-creation of the many French folksongs that Aubert de Gaspé had sprinkled throughout the adventures of Archie and Jules. Roberts' skills as a poet in his own right enables him to bring a French work into the realm of English literature while still trying to be faithful to the nature of the original, an approach that should be kept in mind in comparative studies.

In his introduction to the episodic novel, Roberts discusses the relationship between English and French writing in Canada:

> In Canada there is settling into shape a nation of two races there is springing into existence, at the same time, a literature in two languages. In the matter of strength and stamina there is no overwhelming disparity between the two races. The two languages are admittedly those to which belong the supreme literary achievements of the modern world. In this dual character of the Canadian people and the Canadian literature there is afforded a series of problems which the future will be taxed to solve.[6]

From his post-Confederation perspective Roberts sees one literature in two languages. But this optimistic view does not blind him to the difficulties of such a duality; "a series of problems which the future will be taxed to solve." Several critics have tried to deal with these inherited problems; not least of which is the question of whether Canada has one national literature in two languages or two literatures. Has there been much interchange between anglophone and francophone writing in

Canada? There has been some translation but no Quebec writer of any stature has ever been influenced by an English-Canadian or vice versa. One of the areas that is studied in Comparative Literature is the process of influence, but it is difficult to see how this methodology can apply to the Canadian context.

Roberts came close to the ideal of a Canadian comparatist: a bilingual man of letters. As a writer, poet and the first major translator of French-Canadian writing into English Roberts could argue convincingly for a single Confederation literature. Nineteenth-century-style nationalism in English Canada has often moved in the direction of a single national literature. Roberts' goal, however, is to be achieved not through a bilingual literature but by translating Quebec writing and thus making it English. The dual character of Canadian writing is thus changed into a monolingual literature. Gabrielle Roy's *Bonheur d'occasion* becomes the English novel, *The Tin Flute*, in hundreds of English literature courses.

Despite the use of translations anglophone and francophone writers often function as if the other group did not exist. At the same time immigrant writers are either ignored or swallowed up by one of the majority language groups. When Louis Hémon wrote *Maria Chapdelaine* in 1913 he was religiously trying to follow the tradition of the *roman du terroir*, so much so that it seems to read like a parody of *habitant* piety, so much so that it is often rejected by Quebecois writers as a work that glorifies colonialized Quebec. A more balanced approach would be to read it as the work of an immigrant writer from France. In this narrow nationalistic context it is little wonder that immigrant writers remain invisible and that Stephan Stephansson, Rachel Korn and Georges Bugnet lived, wrote and died in obscurity in Canada.

The development of Canadian Literature in the

past 40 years is part of the post-colonial search for a Canadian identity. Despite the anglophone desire for national unity there is no single history of Canadian writing. There are several histories of French writing: Gérard Tougas' *Histoire de la littérature canadienne-française* (1960), one history each by Roger Duhamel and Gérard Bessette and the four volume opus by Lucien Gélin, Charles Parent and Pierre de Grandpré, *Histoire de la littérature française du Québec* (1967-69). The anglophone history brought out by Carl Klinck, *Literary History of Canada* (1956, 1965 and 1973) deals only with writing in English. What could be called the federalist interpretation of Canadian literary history is, in the final analysis, not supported by the facts of separate literary traditions, or by the work of literary historians.

Recent movements in French-Canadian nationalism and separatism have been supported by Quebec writers who reject the federalist dream and have called their writing *littérature québécoise* so that it will not be confused with *littérature canadienne*. In 1972 when a national association was established to deal with the study of writing in Canada it had to be called, The Association for Canadian and Quebec Literatures.

The paradoxical question — "Can we have one national literature in two languages and with two literary traditions?" — must be reformulated. The existence in Quebec of separatist writers makes it difficult to argue, as did Charles Roberts, for a national "literature in two languages." In this Canadian dilemma we cannot look to the Belgians or Swiss as models because ethnic writing in Canada is not confined to regions or cantons. The interpretation of our national literatures will need to accommodate the history of Canadian critical thought.

During the 1970's much of the commentary on

Canadian writing was preoccupied with the search for unity, with identifying what was distinctively Canadian. One literary critic and writer who tried to deal with the division between English and French writing was Ronald Sutherland. In 1971 Sutherland proposed the theory of the "Mainstream of Canadian Literature":

> What, then, is a sphere of consciousness essentially and peculiarly Canadian? I should think that the main distinguishing feature would have to... dependent upon the main distinguishing feature of the Canadian nation — the coexistence of two major ethnic groups. To be in the emerging mainstream of Canadian literature, therefore, a writer must have some awareness of fundamental aspects and attitudes of both language groups in Canada.
>
> It is just such awareness on the part of a few which is slowly moulding a single, common Canadian mystique out of the previous parallel treads of evolution.[7]

Six years after *Second Image* Sutherland elaborated this thesis in *The New Hero*. While he argued that the central concerns of the mainstream writers were questions of English-French relations and identity he also tried to reassure us that this was a thematic interpretation and "has nothing to do with literary merit."[8] Despite this qualification the thesis is prescriptive and the hierachical scheme has a political basis in which Hugh MacLennan and Roch Carrier are placed at the top of the list of important writers. This thesis emerged from Sutherland's pioneer work in Comparative Canadian Literature and thus appears to have literary origins, but it is nevertheless a federalist view that attempts to include separatist writers, Claude Jasmin and Hubert Aquin, in the unifying mainstream. At the same time it excludes major prairie novelists like Margaret Laurence and Robert Kroetsch and places Sinclair Ross and Morley Callaghan in the tributaries of American literature.

Anglophone critics and academics pursued other

unifying theses for a national literature. Some appear to place borders around Canadian writing in order to distinguish it from both British and American traditions. In *Survival: A Thematic Guide to Canadian Literature*, Margaret Atwood argues that, "The Central symbol for Canada... in both English and French Canadian literature — is undoubtedly Survival, *la survivance*."[9] This controversial reading of Canadian letters is based on the earlier critical work of Northrop Frye, *The Bush Garden*, and D.G. Jones, *Butterfly on Rock*, but moves to the extreme by narrowing the thematic approach to a scheme of four victim positions. Atwood briefly considers three immigrant novels, Marlyn's *Under the Ribs of Death*, Moore's *The Luck of Ginger Coffey*, and Wiseman's *The Sacrifice* (pp. 152-59), but her reading is undercut by the very thesis of the book, "that Canada as a whole is a victim, or an oppressed minority or exploited" (p. 35). By refusing to make any distinction between the immigrant status of Russian Jews in Winnipeg and English-speaking Irish immigrants in Montreal Atwood is distorting reality. The thrust towards a unifying thesis for Canadian writing fails to deal with the minority status not only of French-Canadians but of other ethnic groups as well.

One Quebec critic adopted Sutherland's method of parallel analysis between English and French work. In *La Poésie de frontières* Clément Moisan compares nine pairs of anglophone and francophone poets in order to demonstrate their affinities.[10] The poetry of Atwood, for example, is examined with that of Michèle Lalonde as both reflect the recent movement towards personal liberation. Moisan's study is paradoxical because, while he is supportive of separatist writers, he nevertheless uses comparative methods to present a predominantly centralist view of Canadian writing. This critic uses Atwood's *Survival* to argue that both anglophone and francophone writers share this dominant theme in their work. The linguistic and cultural borders of Moisan's book title are fences between two neighbors, fences that are to be crossed. Moisan's approach, like Sutherland's, is essentially binary and does not include the possibility of a third group.

While D.G. Jones, Northrop Frye and Margaret Atwood consider French writing, to a limited extent, in their unifying studies of Canadian letters, other anglophone critics try to achieve a general view by dealing only with English works. *Patterns of Isolation* by John Moss and *Vertical Man/Horizontal World* by Laurie Ricou demonstrate these narrow readings of Canadian writing.[11] The search for what is distinctively Canadian has been aided by the development of the Canadian mythopoeic school of criticism. One result is that the thematic criticism of Frye, Jones, Atwood, Moss and others has dominated the teaching and the reading of Canadian writing. This thematic approach has been criticized by several authors who find that it has limited many of the possibilities of interpreting our literary traditions. As Paul Stuewe argues in his book, *Clearing the Ground: English-Canadian Literature After Survival*, thematic criticism by its very nature has two major flaws: the statistical fallacy and a tendency towards exclusivity.[12] Careful reading of ethnic writing may help future Canadian critical thought to move out into new directions.

The thematic approach to Canadian letters is closely associated with the environmentalist theses of Canadian history. As Michael Cross explains:

> Frontierism exerted an indirect influence on Canadian historiography which was more widespread that its direct influence. It helped focus attention on the influence of the physical environment on the development of Canadian society, economy and politics. The 'staple theory', perhaps the most im-

portant of all approaches to Canadian history, drew inspiration from Frederick Jackson Turner. The frontier influence remains clear in the staple theory, and in the 'Laurentian school' of Canadian history which grew from the staple theory. These approaches reversed priorities, emphasizing the importance of urban centres rather than frontier outposts. Yet the view of the environment, and even of the role of the frontier, was often similar to that of the Turner thesis. The most striking difference lay in the moral judgements made about the frontier. For Turner, the frontier was the well-spring of all that was good in North American society; for Laurentianists like D.G. Creighton, the frontier was the homeland of parochial farmers who failed to appreciate the commercial dynamism found in cities like Montreal, a dynamism essential for the growth of Canada.[13]

It is ironic that the search for a Canadian interpretation of our history should be based on an imported American thesis, the frontier hypothesis of Wisconsin historian, Frederick Jackson Turner.[14] The geographical determinism found in the writing of A.R.M. Lower and D.G. Creighton had a direct influence on the literary work of Wilfred Eggleston and Northrop Frye.[15] Thematic studies of Canadian writing are predominantly environmentalist interpretations that focus on man's relationship with the natural world around him: the forest, the climate, the plain, the farm. This is often a hostile environment and thus we have the major themes: survival, isolation, exile, death in the snow. Even when these elements are examined as symbols or states of mind as in Margot Northy's *The Haunted Wilderness*, there is the influence of the environmentalist bias.

The central weakness of the environmentalist theses of Canadian history and writing is their intellectual isolationism. The obsession with what is uniquely Canadian diverts the attention of scholarship from the possibilities of comparative social history and comparative literature. Little time has been devoted to examine how Canadian historical development shared features with other countries — the Protestant ethic, industrialization, urbanism, immigration and ethnic heterogeneity. In literature even less work has been done on comparing Canadian writing to that of other countries.[16] Both the view of history and the reading of literature have neglected the institutions, ideas, values and folklore that immigrants brought from Europe and other countries.

The search for a single unifying myth in Canadian writing has its counter parts in the federalist quest for national unity, and in the clear anglocentrism of Canadian History and the anglo-conformism of Canadian Studies. A 1971 editorial in the *Journal of Canadian Studies*, argued against the Federal Government's new multicultural policy because it was a scheme designed "to enlist the widespread support for multiculturalism in the cause of denying the fundamental duality of Canadian society."[17] It seems that the recognition of the other partners in the historic development of Canada may reduce the position of the two founding peoples, especially the English majority who have simply assumed that the major part of newcomers would be counted in their ranks. This nativist attitude in academic circles has tended to discourage prolonged attention to the work of ethnic writers as somehow unpatriotic or at least not a suitable area for study. Because little care was taken with the work of early ethnic writers some of their works were lost and they remained part of an invisible literature. Stephan Stephansson, Mario Duliani and Ivan Danylchuk could have been the beginning of a tradition of ethnic writing in Canada; instead they are all but forgotten.

The lack of reception to what can be called the multicultural dimensions in Canadian letters can be seen in how critics respond to ethnic writers. In the work of Andrew Suknaski the western Canadian elements are emphasised rather than the Ukrainian. Czech novelist,

Josef Skvorecky, is often perceived as a refugee anti-communist writer rather than an artist living in Canada. In the poetry of Pier Giorgio Di Cicco it is the North American perspective that is considered over the Italian. What is the effect of such repeated responses to these writers? I feel, that it is one of self-censorship on the part of the writer. This negative condition has been aggravated by the dominance of thematic criticism. The critical work of Sutherland and Atwood is implicity prescriptive and I suspect has had an influence on younger writers as much as Northrop Frye had on the generation of D.G. Jones and Jay Macpherson. If a writer wants to be read, wants to be taken seriously, he must appear to be Canadian, must become Canadian. The price for the lack of anglo-conformism is the possibility of being marginalized, of being ignored and forgotten.

This fear has its roots in the way ethnic writing has historically been regarded in Canada as quaint, exotic but not important. Ethnic literature has traditionally been defined as writing in the unofficial languages of Canada. In 1935 Watson Kirkconnell edited a collection of ethnic poetry in English translation called, *Canadian Overtones: An Anthology of Canadian poetry written originally in Icelandic, Swedish, Hungarian, Italian, Greek and Ukrainian*.[18] The single Italian in this volume is Liborio Lattoni of Montreal. Thirty six years later little seems to have changed when J. Michael Yates and Charles Lillard published *Volvox: Poetry from the Unofficial Languages of Canada in English Translation*. Again only one Italian-language poet is included, Luigi Romeo, who lived in Canada from 1961 to 1965[19]. A number of Italian-Canadians were writing Italian poetry in the late 1960's and in the 1970's but they are all but invisible. This invisibility is in part due to the assumption that true ethnic writing is in a foreign language. This approach designed to help the ethnic retain his original language also keeps him out of sight from the general population. People with the nationalistic conformist mentality want to believe that if a writer uses English or French he or she has adopted one of the majority cultures and no longer identifies with the ethnic community. The writing of Italian-Canadian authors, in English, French and Italian, challenges these narrow assumptions.

Those who want to marginalize ethnic writing clearly limit it to the unofficial languages. In this view immigrant writers must be assimilated into the anglophone community as quickly as possible for their own good. As one enlightened Canadian writer warns:

> The Jewish and the Asiatic races may prove to be the most recalcitrant as they are highly tradition-oriented, endogamous, and prone to stigmatization. Parliamentary placebos will only cause a contrary atmosphere of cultural quarantine into which out-group Canadians will never be able to enter comfortably as one. Ethnic literature will develop as an artificial by-product of insulated growth, a black cultured pearl, nurtured under the protective shell of Canadian-style tolerance: acceptance without concern. [20]

These are not the words of a racist politician from the 1930's but of Raymond August writing in 1974, and published in *The Canadian Forum*. For this writer there is no place for ethnic writing in Canadian culture. The quaint folk writing of immigrant groups should not be encouraged because the results could be cultural ghettoes and, the boogie man of all anglocentrists, political balkanization. Raymond August goes so far as to deny the validity of the ethnic writer using Canadian material when working in his native tongue:

> The Jewish, Ukrainian, and Icelandic cultural groups in particular make the incongruous assertion of a "Canadian tradition" in their literature — incongruous since the Canadian

tradition has always been English and French in focus and concentration. The inclusion of local colour, Canadian landscapes, Canadian historical personages, or the translation of Canadian poets into the mother tongue and vice versa does not render it as eligible Canadian literature since it fails to activate the evolution of a unique Canadian consciousness. It is surrogate writing, a token of esteem, good will, and so on; a quasi Canadian — quasi old country compromise in descriptions, speech rhythms, sense impression and characterizations that are in fact unreasonable facsimiles of both countries... A Syrian writing about Mount Royal in Arabic is creating Arabic literature; a Syrian writing about Mount Royal in English or French is creating Canadian literature. (p. 11)

Between Watson Kirkconnell and Raymond August we have the two extreme positions that have denied a place for ethnic writing in Canada. The first values this literary expression but only recognizes it as work in the unofficial languages and thus condemns it to oblivion. The second questions the existence of ethnic writing, calls for the use of only English or French and for assimilation as soon as possible. Thus both the friends and enemies of ethnic writing share underlying conformist assumptions. The same nationalism that promoted the development of Canadian literature is now thwarting the development of the multicultural dimension of that literature.[21]

Given this nativist cultural context it is possible to see why Comparative Canadian Literature has not thrived despite the best intentions. The hostility, overt and covert, to ethnic writing has retarded any serious study of this area, to say nothing of the writing and publishing of immigrant authors. Both Comparative Literature and ethnic writing have an internationalist nature: both deal with influences from outside national borders and language barriers; both seek ties with other countries and cultures; both focus on differences as well as similarities. Future scholarship should look to ethnic writing as a way of taking Canadian writing into a truly international context of comparative study and exchange. The broad methodologies of Comparative Literature should be used in the study of ethnic writing and Canadian letters generally.

The language of a work is important but it should be used as only one factor in determining the nature of a piece of writing. To define ethnic literature as writing in the unofficial languages of Canada is to look at the area too narrowly and in a distorted manner. We must consider subject matter, major themes, images, influences, the voice in the work, the role of translation, the author's perspective and possible affiliation. Each individual work must be read and evaluated in terms of these elements. Only then can we determine the sphere of consciousness of the work and the sensibility of the author.

A comparative approach to ethnic literature must deal with a broad spectrum of writing: Walter Bauer's *Fremd in Toronto* and his English work; the Czech novels of Josef Skvorecky; the Italian novels of Maria Ardizzi; the Yiddish poetry of Rachel Korn; and the Spanish work of Naím Nómez. Studies will also include works in English and French that are devoted to immigrant subject matter: Laura G. Salverson's *The Viking Heart* (1923); John Marlyn's *Under the Ribs of Death* (1957); Vera Lysenko's *Yellow Boots* (1954); Joy Kogawa's *Obasan* (1981); F.G. Paci's *The Father* (1984); Marco Micone's *Gens du silence* (1982); Filippo Salvatore's *La Fresque de Mussolini* (1983); and Alexandre Amprimoz's *Sur le damier des tombes* (1983).[22] A working definition of ethnic writing in Canada could be: writing that is concerned with the meeting of two (or more) cultures in which one of the cultures is anglophone or francophone. With this meeting there is often a tension or conflict between the minority culture and the majority one. This definition takes into account immigrant writers whose language is English but whose culture may not be. West Indian writer, Sam Selvon, uses English yet his novels focus on the black man's adjustment to white society. Joy Kogawa's language is English but her novel, *Obasan*, is a personal account of the Japanese experience in Canada during World War II. The internment of Italians in Canada during this war is chronicled in Mario Duliani's French *reportages romancés, La Ville sans femmes*. This flexible model for ethnic literature in Canada will allow us to explore the interrelationships of the writing of various peoples.

In order to study the literary works produced in Canada we must read more than one language and be open to more than one culture. Exposure to ethnic writing is one way to approach the new reality of Multiculturalism. Italian-Canadian literature, as a body of writing, illustrates many of the qualities of a varied ethnic literature in Canada. It exists in three languages: English, French and Italian. While publishing in any of these languages and living in communities from Vancouver to Quebec City, these writers share a common subject matter, the immigrant experience, and demonstrate similar themes and values. The 100 or so active writers do not form one monolithic group or school. On the contrary there is a good deal of diversity in terms of personality, temperament, age, education, social circumstances, and the literary factors of style, genre, perspective, treatment and language. The striking thing is that dispite these disparities and the use of three languages and some dialects, the writers are linked by many elements. It is because of these concrete affinities and not because of a common Italian background that we can speak of an Italian-Canadian literature.

The existence of an ethnic literature such as Italian-Canadian writing, which cuts across language barriers, forces us to review our notions about a national literary tradition and a literary identity. While we cannot deny the fundamental duality of Canadian society, we cannot limit our understanding of that society to a series of binary relationships between anglophone and francophone communities. The goals of political unity and national harmony need not be achieved through linguistic conformity and cultural uniformity. A ferocious nationalism will not protect us from American domination, nor will it result in artistic works of quality. The preoccupation with borders, the postulation of unifying theses of history and literature are relics of a nineteenth-century mentality. The regionalism and the ethnic diversity of this country are realities that must be recognized in the interpretation of our literature.[23]

In Comparative Literature all writing is perceived as being an essential unity, a form of human expression like music, dance or painting. A similar view was expressed by Canadian scholar, Marshall McLuhan when he spoke of a "global village," a human community beyond nationalism. In their imaginative reconstruction of Canadian society as an ethnic mosaic writers have concrete ways of straddling the barriers of time, space and culture. They tell stories to make us real. As Caterina Edwards explains in her novel *The Lion's Mouth*,

> With me, it is always stories. And in the end it is all I can offer you — your story. I recreate your infancy, your childhood, trying to understand. I imagine the bombings, the operation. I look out through your eyes. I become you. I make the story, the book.[24]

NOTES

1 E.D. Blodgett, *Configuration: Essays on the Canadian Literatures* (Toronto: ECW Press, 1982), p. 9.

2 Philip Stratford, "Canada's Two Literatures: A Search for Emblems," *Canadian Review of Canadian Literature* 6 (Spring, 1979), 138.

3 Eli Mandel, "The Ethnic Voice in Canadian Writing," in *Figures in a Ground: Canadian Essays on Modern Literature Collected in Honour of Sheila Watson*, ed. D. Bessai and D. Jackel (Saskatoon: Western Producer Prairie Books, 1978), pp. 264-77.

4 John Moss, *Patterns of Isolation In English Canadian Fiction* (Toronto: McClelland and Stewart, 1974), p. 80.

5 Michael Greenstein, "History in *The Second Scroll*," *Canadian Literature* 76 (Spring, 1978) 37-46. B.W. Powe, *A Climate Charged: Essays on Canadian Writers* (Oakville: Mosaic Press, 1984) described Mordecai Richler as "the Philip Roth of the North."

6 Charles G.D. Roberts, "Introduction," to Philippe Aubert de Gaspé, *Canadians of Old* (Toronto: McClelland and Stewart, 1974), p. 5.

7 Ronald Sutherland, *Second Image: Comparative Studies in Quebec/Canadian Literature* (Toronto: New Press, 1971), p. 124.

8 Ronald Sutherland, "The Mainstream," in *The New Hero: Essays in Comparative Quebec/Canadian Literature* (Toronto: Macmillan of Canada, 1977), p. 93. Cf. D.G. Jones, *Butterfly on Rock: A Study of Themes and Images in Canadian Literature* (Toronto: Univ. of Toronto Press, 1970).

9 Margaret Atwood, *Survival: A Thematic Guide to Canadian Literature* (Toronto: House of Anansi Press, 1972).

10 Clément Moisan, *La Poésie des frontières: Étude comparée des poésies canadienne et québécoise* (LaSalle; Hurtubise HMH, 1979).

11 Laurence Ricou, *Vertical Man/Horizontal World: Man and Landscape in Canadian Prairie Fiction* (Vancouver: Univ. of British Columbia Press, 1973).

12 Paul Stuewe, *Clearing the Ground: English-Canadian Literature After Survival* (Toronto: Proper Tales Press, 1984). See also Frank Davey, "Atwood Walking Backwards," *Open Letter* (Second series) 5 (Summer, 1973), 74-84. and J. Pivato, "Eight Approaches to Canadian Literary Criticism," *Journal of Commonwealth Literature*, Vol. XIII, no. 3 (April, 1979) 43-53.

12 Michael S. Cross, ed., *The Frontier Thesis and the Canadas: The Debate on the Impact of the Canadian Environment* (Toronto: Copp Clark Publishing, 1970), p. 4.

13 Frederick Jackson Turner, "The Significance of the Frontier in American History," in *The Frontier in American History* (New York: Henry Held and Co., 1920), pp. 1-38.

14 A.R.M. Lower, "Geographical Determinants in Canadian History," in *Essays in Canadian Historiography Presented to George Mackinnon Wrong*, ed. Ralph Flenley (Toronto: 1939) and Lower, *Colony to Nation* (Toronto, 1946).

15 Wilfred Eggleston, *The Frontier and Canadian Letters* (Toronto, 1957) and

Northrop Frye, "Conclusion," in *Literary History of Canada: Canadian Literature in English*. ed. Carl F. Klinck (Toronto: University of Toronto Press, 1965), pp. 821-849. See p. 830 for "garrison mentality."

16 The initial work of R.E. Watters, "A Quest for a National Identity: Canadian Literature vis-a-vis the Literature of Great Britain and the United States," *Proceedings of the Third Congress of the International Comparative Literature Association* (The Hague: Mouton, 1962), pp. 224-241, has been followed by only a few published studies: Eva-Marie Kröller, "Water Scott in America, English Canada and Quebec: A Comparison," *Canadian Review of Comparative Literature* 7 (1980), J. Pivato, "Nouveau Roman Canadien," *Canadian Literature* 58 (1973), and M.V. Dimić, "Aspects of American and Canadian Gothicism," in *Actes du VII Congrès de l'Association Internationale de Littérature Comparée* (1979).

17 R.R.H. (Heintzman?), "In the bosom of a single state," *Journal of Canadian Studies* 6, 4 (1971) 1-2, 63-64.

18 Watson Kirkconnell, ed. *Canadian Overtones* (Winnipeg: Columbia Press, 1935).

19 J. Michael Yates, C. Lillard & A.J. West, eds. *Volvox* (Port Clements, B.C.: Sono Nis Press, 1971).

20 Raymond August, "Babeling Beaver hunts for home fire: The place of ethnic literature in Canadian culture," *Canadian Forum* (August, 1974), 8-11. See also Larry Zolf, "How multiculturalism corrupts," *Maclean's* (Nov., 15, 1982).

21 Robert F. Harney, "Ethnic Archival and Library Materials in Canada: Problems of Bibliographic Control and Preservation," *Ethic Forum: Journal of Ethnic Studies and Ethnic Bibliography* 2:2 (Fall, 1982) 3-31. Harney details similar patterns of hostility and neglect with regard to ethnic studies in Canada.

22 See E.D. Blodgett, "Fictions of Ethnicity in Prairie Writing," in *Configuration*, *op. cit.*

23 Dick Harrison, *Unnamed Country: The Struggle for a Canadian Prairie Fiction* (Edmonton: Univ. of Alberta Press, 1977).

24 Caterina Edwards, *The Lion's Mouth* (Edmonton: NeWest Press, 1982), pp. 179-80.

F.G. PACI

Tasks of the
Canadian Novelist Writing
on Immigrant Themes

If we can visualize three concentric circles, we can perhaps simplify this rather imposing title — which seems to read like one of the labours of Hercules. The largest circle would involve the task of the novelist in general. Then there would be the condition of the Canadian writer. And finally the writer on immigrant themes in the smallest circle. This would make us see the relative importance of each circle — and at the same time their relation to each other. In another sense, this tripartite division would give us a static glimpse, however crude, of the dialectical movement that is at play in the novel: the tension between the particular and the universal that resolves itself into the concrete life of the novel.

It must not be forgotten, however, that in the actual experience of writing fiction there is no such abstract division. There is only the fluid whole, with the play of particular and universal forces constantly modifying it.

It is also important to emphasize that nothing is presented here as a hard and fast rule. Hercules performed his labours one way. There could have been other ways. And each writer learns best from trial and error which methods work for him. There is no compensating for the writing experience. I offer only guidelines that have been learned only after much groping in the dark. They have too often not been realized in my own work. Some of us do not have the inborn strengths of a Hercules and must toil away with ordinary strength.

There are basically five tasks of the novelist in general, but they can be summarized into one statement:

to present Reality. Note: not "reality," which carries with it the notion of realism in the novel — and also a verisimilitude to the popular conception of the "real" world. Realism is a much wider conception, including within it, for example, fantasy and the marvellous. The Real is the truth, and the truth is the whole. Big words, but that is the way it goes.

D.H. Lawrence, who cannot be trusted in all matters, nevertheless offers us a good starting point in clarifying the importance of the novel. In "Why a Novel Matters," he says:

> The novel is the one bright book of life. Books are not life. They are only tremulations on the ether. But the novel as a tremulation can make the whole man alive tremble. Which is more than poetry, philosophy, science, or any other book — tremulation can do.[1]

Lawrence is speaking of affecting or capturing the "whole man alive," instead of just part of him. In other words, the novel should address itself to the complete human being by being about the complete human being; that is, man as a composite of head, heart, and crotch — the principal zones of influence. But the novel should be even more encompassing than this. For it should include thanatos as well as eros. It includes, for example, the nihilism of a Samuel Beckett — and such disparate writers as Peter Handke and Thomas Pynchon and Alain Robbe-Grillet. It includes the *not-alive* as well. And the fantastic and marvellous and surrealistic. Lawrence was too busy beating his own breast for eros (in the original Greek conception of *life*) to see that the novel should also encompass its negative — the destructive and nihilistic elements in the human psyche that spring from thanatos (the death instinct). The novel includes the whole — the negative as well as the positive.

What is real to most people is what is tangible, verifiable, commonsensical, functional, secure, logical — the everyday world in which we make our living, raise our families, and worship our idols. In this world we live on a bumpy road of surface reality and abstract reality. There are clear separations — and the law of identity reigns. It is a dualistic world of mind and body, lust and love, spirit and flesh, heart and mind, reality and illusion. Scientific thinking pervades this world (going back to Bacon and Descartes). We live our concrete everyday lives — and the irony of it all is that we base our truths on abstractions. All duality and separation is abstraction — when taken for the whole. Reality, on the other hand, includes and goes beyond all this. Reality is the reconciliation of all dualities. For this Reality only the whole is the truth. Every reality is only a part of the truth — is merely one myth among others. But this Reality sees the unity and distinction of all the parts. It is materialism and idealism, phenomenology and existentialism, behaviourism and innatism, holism and dualism, Marxism and capitalism. For this Reality there is something else besides what exists. What exists lives and passes away. What is real endures. But what is Real encompasses them both — the existential and the essential, the outer and the inner, the physical and the metaphysical — encompasses them both in their difference and identity, in their constant dialectic, in their wholeness. This Reality goes beyond the old controversies in the novel between realism and naturalism, form and content, solipsism and correspondence. It goes beyond precise rendition of detail and a cataloguing of "everything" — and it is as much divorced from the correspondence with reality as fantasy and the marvellous. On the other hand, it is as selective as any artistic form filtered through a sensibility. It is imitative and non-imitative. But it never shrinks to the sensibility of the writer alone. It keeps its connection — its interplay and dialectic — with the objective. The subject-object connection, although strained and pulled either way, cannot be broken, for neither can *be* without the other. If the writer only plays with words, if he is only concerned with form and technique, then he is in danger of cutting away the objective — the existent — and is undercutting the fundamental purpose of his medium, language. Language in itself is not Real. Just as one human being in himself is not Real. Language is relation. The human being is a Being-in-the-world, to use a Heideggerian term. He is as much defined by what he is not as by what he is. The negative cannot be separated from the positive. Me and Not-me are different and the same. Reality goes beyond logic and says a thing can be A and not-A at the same time. Logic divides and sees everything as static. It is typified by the epigram to G.E. Moore's *Principia Ethica*: Everything is what it is, and not another thing. But this is only a half-truth. Reality and life are one and whole, and include time and change, so that at the point that something is what it is, it is also not what it is; that is, it is changing into something else. Identity and difference pervade Reality. What is paradoxical to commonsense logic is laughed at by Reality. Life goes on in spite of all the artificial abstractions. In spite of Zeno's paradox, the arrow reaches the target. The moment of our birth is the moment of our death.

Reality in the novel can be summarized by the emptiest of Hegel's mediations: Being plus Nothingness resolve themselves into Becoming.

So the Reality we are speaking about includes all differences — all parts — because it sees that only the whole is the truth. A scientist explains how the atom functions, appealing to our intellects — our need for a comprehensible pattern with which we can tame the forces of Nature. But this is a myth because it is only a part of the whole. A philosopher explains the metaphysical essence of our being, appealing to our minds. And this is a myth. A poet writes a lyrical ballad with images that appeal to the heart, the eye, the ear, and the instinctive underpinnings of language — which may go as deep as the collective unconscious. And this is a myth. But the novelist must see all these aspects of reality. He must try for the whole; not only man alive, as Lawrence saw it, but man dead, and man dreaming, and man thinking, and man killing, and man making love. And he can do it by caring deeply about his material, by creating a detailed world within the covers of his book, by making each character live on his own terms, by thinking in images, and lastly by capturing that indefinable magic that makes everything work in harmony. Just as Shakespeare did. Just as Tolstoy did. By losing themselves in it. By Negative Capability. By self-abnegation.

But just when we think we can capture Reality or — in this case — life, along comes the voice of commonsense which instantly bursts our balloon. In speaking about writing his first novel, *The Mountain and the Valley*, Ernest Buckler says:

> If there is any purgatory more undiluted than attempting to trap the quicksilver of life with the laggard spring of words, I don't know it. You so often feel like those fatuous ancients who thought to enclose the bird with a wall. For life is so infinitely tangential. It flees touch like a ball of mercury flees the finger. And you find not its smallest feature in clear-outline, but always in solution. And so dauntingly various. *War and Peace* is alleged to have said everything about everything. But it doesn't... The greatest novel ever written is a mere phrase, a word, a letter, if you like, in the infinite language of human relations.[2]

And Buckler is right, of course. We always try: we never make it. The very nature of writing, as a matter of fact, is a turning away from life, a sort of *non-life* of putting

41

one word after another, changing them around, trying to say exactly what we mean — and never getting there. How many of us, for example, can describe *exactly* what a person looks like? The whole experience of writing fiction is the Negative Way, the Via Dolorosa. We think of Marcel Proust in his cork-lined room on the boulevard Haussmann or Flaubert ensconced in Croisset or Kafka bug-like in his parents' home. How can we put our finger on the quicksilver when we have turned our backs on it? If we want to capture life, why do we not live it, for God's sake! Because all comprehension is negation. In order to understand we must step back and look from a distance. We must ponder, mull over, analyse, break down, reflect — in short, think. But all these forms of thinking are abstractions, negations. A novelist must go beyond them — while including them — and recapture the original wholeness of being. Every novelist is an ontologist — and if the novel is a middle class art form, then he is a bourgeois ontologist.

And this brings us to another important consideration if we are speaking of the novel in general: its historical roots. Writers like Defoe and Richardson started out by giving us an illusion of reality — everyday reality. In the case of Defoe, his verisimilitude or "fake autobiography" was so authentic that *Robinson Crusoe, A Journal of the Plague Year*, and *Moll Flanders* were believed outright. The novel, in opposition to the Romance and Epic, Hawthorne maintained, "is presumed to aim at a very minute rendition of the possible and probable in the ordinary course of human experience."[3] Ian Watt in *The Rise of the Novel* maintains that individual experience began with the novel to "replace collective tradition as the ultimate arbiter of reality."[4] With the novel there arose the importance of the individual consciousness — the individual as important in himself — a reality indebted as much to Rousseau and Kant and Locke as it was to the French Revolution. And with the individual consciousness there ran parallel the idea of getting at the exact truth of experience, a conception that is very much connected to empiricist and Enlightenment thinking:

> The autobiographical memoir, the epistolary method, the dramatized consciousness, the withdrawal of the author from the scene, the stream of consciousness; all these methods are designed to heighten the desired effect of authenticity and verisimilitude by locating experience in the individual consciousness, and by making that consciousness operate in a particular place at a particular time.[5]

This authenticity to events and withdrawal of the author point to empiricism's emphasis on the object of scrutiny. It led to scientific realism — the need to include as much as humanly possible (Balzac's *La Comédie humaine*) and then to the naturalist school with Zola.

But all along there were rumblings of discontent with this slavery to the object. Novelists like Emily Brontë and Dostoevsky — and even the supreme realist, Flaubert — enlarged the scope of the novel to include the marvellous and fantastic. But the object all along was to create a *reality* more vivid than reality itself:

> The realist, if he is an artist, will seek to give us not a banal photographic representation of life, but a vision of it that is fuller, more vivid and more compellingly truthful than even reality itself.[6]

To the point in the 20th century when the novel swings back to the subject of consciousness in Joyce and Woolf:

> Life is not a series of gig lamps symmetrically arranged; life is a luminous halo, a semi-transparent envelope surrounding us from the beginning of consciousness to the end. Is it not the

task of the novelist to convey this varying, this unknown and uncircumscribed spirit, whatever aberration or complexity it may display, with as little mixture of the alien and external as possible?[7]

Yet there is an instinctive repulsion for the extremities of Joyce (*Finnegans' Wake*) and Woolf (*The Waves*) — that they severed the subject-object connection and tried to create a community of consciousness (Woolf) and a cosmological consciousness (Joyce) without anchoring them in a particular consciousness. The universal by itself is empty without the concrete. The *halo* can be so bright as to blind us to what it is supposed to illuminate. As the phenomenologists say, consciousness is always consciousness of something.

Later in the century proponents of the *nouveau roman* like Robbe-Grillet tried to efface metaphor and subjectivism altogether to create a novel of scientific objectivity. Back to the object, in other words.

Which brings us back to the Realism of the novel, or its inherent tendency to present the *whole* as a never-ending dialectic between subject and object, fantasy and reality, the irrational and the rational, spirit and matter, feeling and abstraction, the particular and the universal. For it is the dialectical flux, or mediation, between all these dualities which constitutes the Real.

All this is fine and good, but it is still too abstract and theoretical. How do we try to present the Real? Anyone can present theory. How do we put it into practice?

First, by caring about our material. Not by having a mild interest, or a burning curiosity — or by feeling that the material is relevant or that it will reach millions of people. And certainly not to make money, although we will take any that comes our way. But to feel a need at the roots of our being, a need that consumes us consciously and unconsciously, intellectually and emotionally. In order to know when to speak, we must know when to be silent. We must know when to wait, when to let experience and reaction and interpretation settle like sediment into the bottom of the psyche.

Resonance and deep texture in fiction come from deeply felt experience. Usually we care about content first and then about the best possible form to display it in. Again subject and object. When most of us start to write fiction we imitate those who have influenced us. We are not so much concerned with the concrete as the play of words, the haunting power of language. We are like apprentices who are still marvelling at the tools of the trade. We are carried along by the passion and the power of words. We write of personal experiences with Faulkner's voice or Joyce's voice or Beckett's voice. We are infatuated with language; its look, its smell, its taste, its power. But it is all a hollow bravado, a castle of cards, a still-life photograph of words. There is no life in what we write. We are too concerned with form and technique and the odour of our own vomit — and we cannot see past our noses.

But when we really start to care for what we are writing about, instead of getting high on our verbal flourishes or the mere look of the words on paper, we see how we are each rooted in a particular time and a particular place — and we start to render the material as honestly as possible. Then our task becomes to combine plain speaking with authentic emotion. Plain speaking comes from the ability to de-create the *I*, the ego, and to see people and things exactly as they are, without interference. It is the eradication of all affectation, insincerity, and self-importance. As Wittgenstein believed, a writer should have the veracity that will not permit his tone to be louder or softer than his feelings by as much as a single vibration.[8] He should aim for a perfect fit between emotion and its expression — where each word is tested for its true weight. If the writer does this well enough he might be lucky to experience a fusion between himself and his material — a fusion of subject and object. The writer becomes the vehicle of the object. Language and Reality utter themselves.

If this is the case for the novel in general, it is also true for the Canadian novel, as Ernest Buckler's commonsense voice reminds us again:

> If you're a Canadian, and write as honestly as you can about what you know — here or anywhere else — and the result doesn't sound Canadian — well, no conscious attitude you strike will ever make it sound so. If you're a Canadian and want to write a distinctly Canadian novel, I'd say just trust your natural processes, Mac, just trust your natural processes. Don't *try* to write *like* anything — except yourself.[9]

We should be true to our time and place — as simple as that. We should not try to emulate the British or the Americans, although we can certainly learn a great deal from them. It is a very difficult situation to be in: caught between these two cultures with the same language, constantly fed their literature and values, and feeling inferior to both. The natural rhythms of the British and American consciousness cannot help but creep in. Both have a longer tradition to work from, both are more confident of themselves, both have very high standards — nevertheless, we must be true to our time and place. We must speak in the Canadian idiom. We must make the zones of influence — the head, the heart, and the crotch — speak Canadian. For those of us too used to reading of these zones in other idioms, in the task is not easy. Someone like Margaret Laurence, however, has done an admirable job in this respect. So we have some writers to learn from and build on. Let us stop looking to New York and London for the stamp of approval, for God's sake. This has been said over and over, but it bears repeating: No one will respect our sensibility unless we respect it ourselves.

Yet even more particular than caring about time and place is the care for the individual experiences that have nurtured us. For me, it is the immigrant experience — the central theme of my background. For someone else it could be the loss of innocence, or familial love, or the rise of political consciousness. Whatever it is, though, this is the individual aspect of the novel — its core — the mediation of the universal and particular; where it gets its concrete life.

It was a trip to Italy, my first back in twenty years since my parents emigrated when I was four, that dramatically made me aware that I had to come to terms with my background and the tangle of emotions it had engendered. *Emotions* is the key word. Tolstoy speaks in a more inclusive vein:

> Art is a human activity consisting in this, that one man consciously, by means of certain external signs, hands on to others feelings he has lived through, and that other people are infected by these feelings and also experience them.[10]

This is what I had failed to understand about fiction — the transmission of deeply felt experience. That one had to dig deep in his own self. That one had to deal with the old scars and the festering wounds. That one had to make peace with the old ghosts.

So the things I deeply felt about began to emerge in my fiction as I was writing *The Italians*, my first novel on immigrant themes. And more so in *Black Madonna* and *The Father*. Some of these were the self-sacrifice of the first-generation immigrant parents, the painful clash between *la via vecchia* (the old way) and *la via nuova* (the new way), the simple life of immigrant Italians as opposed to the glamorized criminal life depicted in the US media and literature, the loss of the old language by the second generation, the emotional barriers between generations, the hard-working lives of the parents, the strength of family ties, and the indomitable spirit of these people in uprooting themselves and starting all over in a foreign culture. These were the concrete sources of my emotional make-up. I had something that I cared about deeply and something worth writing about. I had something to tell other people. How was I going to go about doing it?

I began to see, for one, that a novelist had to create a believable and vivid world which absorbed the reader's interest. In an essay originally published in 1925 José Ortega y Gasset expressed it well for all of us:

> ... the author must begin by luring us into the closed precinct that is his novel and then keep us there cut off from any possible retreat to the real space we left behind. ... The author must build around us a wall without chinks or loopholes through which we might catch, from within the novel, a glimpse of the outside world. ... no writer can be called a novelist unless he possesses the gift of forgetting, and thereby making us forget, the reality beyond the walls of his novel.[11]

In his *Lectures on Literature* Vladimir Nabokov refers to this ability to create a separate believable world within the covers of the book as the ability to enchant; that is, to create a spell that will pull the reader into the world of the book.[12] And the world of the book need not necessarily be a realistic world. It may be divorced from the real world — a science fiction world, a wish-fulfillment world, and so on. As a matter of fact, no matter how close or how far it is to the real world — if it is a first-rate novel — the novel's world will be an entirely different world. The unwritten lines to all novels are: Let us pretend. It is the creation of a separate Real world. It is not the novelist's business to tell a true story. He is a deceiver, an enchanter, who conspires with Nature, or the real, to spin a tale. But whatever world he is creating, it should be a vivid one, clear and specific. The reader should be made to see things clearly, as well as have his other senses activated. Here detail and precision of statement come in. Here — even if time and place skip along wildly or characters speak and act oddly — the reader has to be made to feel that the author is in sure control of things.

If we look at some of the tradition in Canadian literature on immigrant themes, we see that there is usually the creation of two worlds: the old and the new. Whether one is trying to cope with the new world with an old world sensibility as Susanna Moodie does, for example, in *Roughing It in the Bush*, or one forsakes the old for the new values as in *Under the Ribs of Death*, or one tries to beat the new world as its own game as in *The Apprenticeship of Duddy Kravitz*, there is a schizophrenia at work, a teetering between two worlds, and a painful amount of psychic scarring as a result. In a large sense Margaret Atwood is right when she says all Canadians are immigrants at heart.[13] The immensity of the land defeats us. We praise its grandeur like Moodie, but at the same time hate living in it. We assume its values and identity like Sandor Hunyadi in *Under the Ribs of Death* but at the same time refute our heritage and humanism.

I wrote my first three novels on immigrant themes unaware of the tradition behind me. I had not read Marlyn or Moodie or Wiseman or Kreisel. I also believed that *The Italians* was the first full-length novel on Italian immigrant themes. Not having anything to build on or learn from, I had to depend on my own resources. This had its advantages as well as its disadvantages. I had to forge my own path, for one, but I had no guiding paths to keep me from going astray. Actually, I was not so much writing novels on immigrant themes as novels about certain families who happened to be of Italian descent. The family was the major focus. Therefore, the worlds I tried to create were those of the Gaetano's and Barone's and Mancuso's — principally within their homes and in the Italian neighbourhood of the West End, which includes their places of work. The conflict of cultures and values, consequently, is conducted within the family itself — between the parents and the second generation. It is a rather closed-off world — a cocoon-like world of the house and the buffer of the immediate Italian neighbourhood. As a matter of fact, *Black Madonna* principally concerns itself with what happens when the cocoon-like world and the buffer of the neighbourhood dissolve around Assunta Barone — the Italian widow who has not adapted at all to the new country. In *The Father*, Oreste Mancuso can be said to take a further step than Assunta. He can survive outside the life of his home, but not outside the life of his neighbourhood. Of course, we are dealing with states of soul as well as places. And here the details of these worlds must be meticulously recorded. The sights and smells of a small city hockey arena. The bravado of a high school dance. The theatrical solemnity of a parish procession. The grime and grit and heat of a steel plant. The warmth and coziness of a neighbourhood bakery. Here selection of detail is more important than inclusiveness. Small things, like the way steel plant workers blow out flue dust from their noses. Or the springy sticky feel of bread dough. One asks: Why this attention to detail? Because it is all the same thing. One cares about the material enough to bring it to life for a reader. One cares about his characters enough that he has to give them a world of their own. One must make images speak instead of ideas. One must try to capture the magic. It is all one and the same thing — the need to get it right, to present Reality.

And if Reality is the subject in connection with the object, we have to look at the other side of the dialectic as well. If the object is the world, then the subject is of course the character. The character is defined just as much by what he is not as by what he is. The outer defines him as much as the inner. The negative pervades Reality. But if the novel has a traditional emphasis, it's surely the importance of character, of a unique state of consciousness — of the inner human being. The novel can be said to have come into existence, as a matter of fact, on the strength of the ordinary character — of ordinary consciousness being the interpreter of reality.

So the task of the novelist here is to make characters live in their own right. It is to give each person who enters the novel, no matter how inconsequential, the dignity of being clearly seen and identified in some way. It is almost as if writing fiction were a moral activity. The great writers are usually the ones who have negated themselves to let their characters live. Look for Shakespeare in his work and you will not find him. Faulkner was as pleased to have created Jason Compson, a character whom he loathed, as Dilsey in *The Sound and the Fury*. Flaubert writes to Colet that he has had to be in the skins of characters for whom he feels aversion in *Madame Bovary*. Tolstoy did not exactly like Vronsky but was pretty fair with him. Mark Twain lets Huckleberry Finn speak for himself, in his idiom and sensibility. In creating such characters the authors step back and allow other voices to be heard. It is a quieting of the ego with its quirks and biases and convictions and letting another human being entirely different come to life. It is making the language and the images serve the characters. It is Keats's Negative Capability. And if pushed far enough it can even be the road of the mystic — or the sublimation of self leading to the individual being engulfed by the Universal. This has been one of the principal avenues to mystical experience from Meister Eckhart to Saint John of the Cross to Jacob Boehme to

Simone Weil. Many people might argue vehemently against this, but writing can be construed as prayer.

Nevertheless, I would agree that the novelist cannot go too far on this road. He has to be in control. He has to keep his wits about him. He has to maintain his distance, his disinterestedness. And yet —. There can also be a merger, a magical merger — if the writer has given himself authentically up to his characters — when he loses himself to the characters and the life of the book. The book begins to write itself. The characters assume a life of their own. The writer feels he is just a vehicle. The book belongs to the characters. Again it is the fusion of subject and object — novelist and book, writer and language, writer and character — where the characters utter themselves.

If we want a guide in Canadian literature for the creation of character we need go no further than Margaret Laurence. Here is a tradition and a set of high standards to learn from. From her African characters to her three sets of generations in *The Stone Angel, A Jest of God, The Fire-Dwellers*, and *The Diviners* she has brought to life human beings any country would be proud to have in its literature. She has given them their proper idiom, given them their time and place, and bestowed all her care and love on them. If there is any ingredient necessary for the creation of character it is compassion. Compassion (from *com* — with and *passio* L. — suffering) means to be able to sympathize with those who suffer. But we can broaden its meaning somewhat by saying it is to "co-feel" any emotion — joy, anxiety, happiness, pain — with another human being. It is the art of emotional telepathy — and some, like Eckhart, would say it is the highest of the virtues. And this is not a compassion that slides into sentimentality and maudlin writing. It is a compassion that "feels," but at the same time is tempered with iron-fair judgement. Bad fiction perpetuates illusion. Authentic fiction unmasks illusion. Not the illusion of dreams and fantasy, which is part of Reality and which enriches it, but that of distortion and superficiality and easy half-truth which pass off for something they are not. Illusion, bad or good, is encompassed by Reality — it cannot pass for Reality.

In my own fiction the task has always been to give flesh and blood to mere skeletons. It is difficult to express exactly how characters emerge. They are a result of so many factors: a sentiment, an image, an old memory, an idea, a composite of two or more real-life people. As mentioned above, *The Italians* started simply as an account of a family who just happened to be of Italian descent. There was no intention of writing on immigrant themes. These things simply emerged in the writing. I had certain characters in mind drawn from my own life and from imagination, as well as a definite place and time. But novels often end up very different from what they were first intended to be. Gradually, in the writing, it dawned on me that I was celebrating people of my father's generation who had immigrated to a new country. Specifically, they were the hardworking semi-skilled or unskilled labourers who came over mostly for the sake of their families and went unnoticed all their lives. I had worked in the steel plant and had seen them at work. The disparity between their lives on the job and their lives at home struck me forcefully. While their sons and daughters were enjoying the comforts of the Affluent Society in the Sixties, they were slaving away — ignored by the media and literature. It was about time that someone wrote of them fairly. But the weakness of this is that the characters tend to be used for an ulterior purpose — which will not do. In *Black Madonna* the characters are more true to themselves. They exist for themselves alone. I had felt in *The Italians* that I had been unfair in rendering the mother of the Gaetano family, so I went about trying to tell an Italian immigrant mother's story. Certain images played a decisive role in creating Assunta Barone — but the predominant one was of the black-clad old Italian widows I used to see often in church when I was a boy. They were mysterious and primitive and scary to me, like black harbingers of death. Oreste Mancuso in *The Father* came about in a very roundabout way. I originally had the characters of Stephen and Michael Mancuso in mind and intended to write of them in the present time. But along the way the idea of a trilogy of novels came to mind, a trilogy tracing their lives through three stages — past, present, and future. So *The Father* was supposed to have simply presented their backgrounds. However, the more I wrote the more their relationship with their father came to the fore. In each successive draft Oreste took on more and more layers of flesh and blood. He virtually wrote himself into the book. He achieved an importance I had never envisaged. I did not know how much I cared about him until I finished writing. I did not know how much he would rise above the ideas and images that at one time tended to suffocate the life of the characters.

Images should serve character, true, but they are also important in universalizing the individual and the concrete. The task of the novelist, then, is to create a proper tension between what to say and what not to say. To show and not to tell, in other words. Too much explanation is like too many weeds that choke the life of the novel. If a picture is worth a thousand words, then a word-picture is worth perhaps nine hundred and ninety-nine.

A good exponent of minimalism in prose writing is Ernest Hemingway. Here is an excerpt from "The Art of the Short Story," which was supposed to have been a preface for a collection of stories:

> A few thing I have found to be true. If you leave out important things or events that you know about, the story is strengthened. If you leave or skip something because you do not know it, the story will be worthless. The test of any story is how very good the stuff is that you, not your editors, omit.[14]

This guideline can be used for the novel as well, although if done improperly can lead to mannerism, as in some of Hemingway's own works. C.M. Bowra in his *Ancient Greek Literature* gives a more useful guideline for all prose writers:

> ... Greek literature achieves its special distinction by omitting everything that is not essential to the plan of the whole; and securing its effect by the power given to each part in its place. The Greeks had a sure instinct for what was really significant, and they omitted everything else... Greek prose is normally concise and often simple. Truths of great acuteness and situations of real moment are expressed with such directness that at first we are puzzled and feel that it is almost childish. Then we realize that this is another aspect of the Greek desire to state the essential and nothing more. On the whole they disliked fine writing, and for all its subtlety and power their prose seems to avoid anything except its proper purpose of conveying information. But behind the austere exterior lies a reserve of strength. The simplest words may yield a profound truth and an emotion which is all the stronger for being disciplined.[15]

This "reserve of strength" can apply to what Hemingway is speaking about as well. It is the strength in the prose that comes from the tension of leaving out the unessentials (and in Hemingway's case, the essentials) — the strength produced by the constant tension between what to say and what not to say. What not to say can be often more important than what to say. Passing over something in silence, to use Wittgenstein's famous last line in the *Tractatus*, can make it sound louder than all the talk of ages. Again the negative. Seeing that often the negative is as powerful in rendering Reality as the positive.

Greek prose style can be said to combine plain speaking with noble sentiment — and this can be of aid to any writer. In this age when the Word has been tarnished and maltreated by mass culture and mass media we have lost the reverence for language. In many respects, language has become a means of "covering over" rather than un-covering and dis-covering. Consequently, being direct and honest can often be construed as being naive and childish. If language is the House of Being, as Heidegger maintained, then we would prefer one built on rock. One more helpful guideline that the Greeks can provide prose stylists is from their motto for science: *Sozein ta Phainomena*, to preserve things as they show themselves to be.

Learning to speak plainly, to capture the strength and deep idioms of the English language, is not easy. One has to go back and read the great stylists like Swift, Dryden, Addison and Steele, Keats (letters), and Byron (prose). Then the Canadian writer has to go back to his own tradition to pick up the Canadian idiom. He should try to see where the British idiom starts to change into a Canadian one. And then, in more modern writing, where the American idiom has crept in. If this is all poppycock, then he should simply keep his ear open, heed Buckler's advice, trust to his instincts, and be as honest as possible. The thing is, not to fake it. To try to be attentive to one's place and time. But all writers are readers. Just as one cannot paint in the avant garde unless he has mastered the tradition, so too one cannot advance the use of language unless one has mastered past usage. James Joyce, for example, rings with the resonance of past literature — and not only of the English.

To render images precisely and to let them speak

instead of ideas — this is actually equitable to the sensibility of the writer. And, again, to not expatiate one's ideas, to not let mannerism and show-off writing creep into one's prose, to preserve things as they show themselves to be — all this involves the negating of the novelist's self. Negative Capability. While the scientist talks about the flower, the writer must be the flower. Knowledge and being are one only through the power of the negative.

In trying to render the immigrant experience certain images were used — not all of them very successful, I might add. The writer cannot be too self-conscious in choosing images and symbols. They must already "be there", so to speak — or be organically part of the story. Images and symbols have to be open-ended. They should reach into the darkness of myth and archetype, into such depths where no words can follow. One image that seemed to arise naturally from the story was the trousseau trunk in *Black Madonna*. As a thing in itself it seemed credible. Immigrant mothers take trousseau trunks with them to the new country and accumulate things for their daughters' marriages. It is a natural link between a mother and daughter — something from the old world is passed on to a new generation of the new world. But in *Black Madonna* there are problems in the rites of passage, just like those encountered by Parsifal in his search for the Holy Grail — and beyond that the trunk must speak for itself.

The last guideline for writing novels is the most difficult to explain. What does it mean, to capture the magic? Does it mean to capture the pulse of life in words? To capture authentic emotion and infect the reader with it? To enchant the reader and make his spine tingle? Or is it to be carried along, as in a trance, by a superior force that transcends rationality and intuition? Is it to capture a slice of Reality unwittingly, so that no matter how many times your book is read it will still be like quicksilver? Or is it all of these?

Certain books read at certain times in our lives seem to have this magic quality. They seem to open the doors of consciousness wider, letting in fresh, heady air. *The Sound and the Fury*, for example, has had this effect on people. So has *Ulysses* and *Wuthering Heights* and *The Great Gatsby* and *Anna Karenina* and *The Brothers Karamazov*. There is something about these books, an indefinable magic, that springs out at us and captures our heads and hearts. We read them again and again. The snap and crackle of the initial flame has softened, yes, but the flame still burns.

What have these novels got that other fairly good books do not? They have undoubtedly captured memorable characters. They have also created their own worlds. There are clear evocations of time and place — along with the haunting images and obsessive emotions and the stirring language. But what is that extra quality that sets them apart? I do not know. But I imagine it has something to do with all these things working in the right way — the book showing us what consciousness is really like and giving us a wider glimpse of what it means to be a human being.

All novels, in the end, have to do with sensibility — with the heart wedded to the mind (and the lurking presence of the crotch). This sensibility, this feeling and compassion that is joined with disinterest and artistic distance, is the cement of the novel. It holds everything together, gives it force and character. It is implicit in the care for material, in the creation of a separate world, in the deference to characters and images, and lastly in the harmony that is achieved in subserving all these parts to the whole. Writing novels has to do with play — with arranging toys in a pattern, with creating some sort of meaning out of the apparent chaos of the world. This playing, in the end, releases joy because it is as if human beings have the gift of magic. We are co-creators. We love life. And we want to extend it.

But I also imagine that this magic has to do with the author ripping away part of his soul to write his novel. And that he is never the same afterwards. Sometimes the author may not even know that this is happening during composition. But a month afterwards, maybe a year, or even two, he will wake up and know.

So what matters more than the fact that a novelist is a Canadian or an immigrant is that he has created a good book that adds something to life. That the book perhaps can be read over and over and enrich the lives of other people. That maybe twenty and fifty years down the road some person in a small town will pick it up in the local library and experience a moment of revelation. Because the part of the soul that was ripped out to write the book will still be warm, will still be breathing.

NOTES

1 D.H. Lawrence, *Phoenix*, ed. Edward MacDonald (New York: Viking Press, 1964), p. 535.

2 Ernest Buckler, "My First Novel," in *Ernest Buckler*, ed. Gregory Cook (Toronto: McGraw-Hill Ryerson, 1972), p. 22.

3 Nathaniel Hawthorne, "Preface" to *The House of the Seven Gables* in *Novelists on the Novel*, ed. Miriam Allott (New York: Columbia U. Press, 1966), p. 51.

4 Ian Watt, *The Rise of the Novel* (Berkeley, 1957), p. 14.

5 Miriam Allott, *Novelists on the Novel* (New York: Columbia, 1966), p. 24.

6 Guy de Maupassant, "Le Roman," Introduction to *Pierre et Jean* (1888) in Allott, p. 71.

7 Virginia Woolf, "Modern Fiction," *The Common Reader* in Allott, p. 77.

8 Ricarda Huch, in speaking of Gottfried Keller in *Letters from Ludwig Wittgenstein*, ed. Paul Engelmann, trans. L. Furtmuller (Oxford: Basil Blackwell, 1967), p. 86.

9 *Op. cit.*, Buckler, p. 26.

10 Leo Tolstoy, *What Is Art?*, trans. Almyer Maude (New York: Bobbs-Merrill, 1960), p. 51.

11 José Ortega y Gasset, *The Dehumanization of Art*, trans. Helene Weyl (New Jersey: Princeton, 1968), p. 91-92.

12 Vladimir Nabokov, *Lectures on Literature*, ed. Fredson Bowers (New York: Harcourt Brace Jovanovich, 1980), p. 5.

13 Margaret Atwood, "Afterword" to *The Journals of Susanna Moodie* (Toronto: Oxford Press, 1970), p. 62.

14 Ernest Hemingway, "The Art of the Short Story," *Paris Review*, Anniversary Edition (1981), p. 88.

15 C.M. Bowra, *Ancient Greek Literature* (London: Oxford Press, 1967), p. x.

C.D. MINNI

The Short Story
as an Ethnic Genre

> I was looking at the back of a new dollar bill, at the scene of
> somewhere on the prairies, and all of a sudden I was looking
> right through it and I wasn't in Toronto at all any more — I
> was back out west.[1]

That is how Robert Kroetsch's short story "That Yellow
Prairie Sky" begins. I chose this example at random to
demonstrate what I mean by the recurrent elements in
the Canadian short story of which ethnic writing is a
native hybrid.

In Kroetsch's story, the first person narrator remembers his life as a prairie wheat farmer, when pros-
perity and dreams were at the whim of Nature. The first
sentence establishes a nostalgic mood, and although the
character never describes his life in the big city, we sense
that he feels out of place there. He is an outsider, almost
as if a part of him has remained on the farm.

Such is the surface plot, but there are undercurrents
of emotion to this story. Perceptive readers know, without being specifically told, that the narrator 1. is lonely,
2. is nostalgic, 3. feels exiled from his roots, 4. suffers
from an identity crisis, 5. has feelings of inexplicable
regrets, 6. has different values, and 7. has a different
viewpoint.

My argument is this: that the short story, at its best,
always deals with outside figures like Kroetsch's narrator — what I will call marginal people. They are characters who feel isolated because their emotional terms of
reference are different. Immigrants fall easily into such
a category, and so perhaps not surprisingly the ethnic

short story (which for the purpose of this article will emphasize Italo-Canadian writing) is a particularly good example of my thesis.

The most common theme — by corollary — is alienation.

A leisurely tour through a cross-section of recent short story writing in Canada will prove both points.

Consider another random example, Caterina Edwards' story "The Last Young Man."[2] In it, Maria marries Beppi after a brief courtship and immigrates with him to Canada. He is a good man, but she does not love him. She marries him because her father has arranged the marriage, after properly checking him out, and in their small rural Italian village a daughter does not oppose her parents' wishes in such matters.

Beppi takes her to Edmonton, to his rickety house, the basement of which he rents to boarders from his native village. They treat her with kindness and respect, and during long winter evenings entertain her with stories of home.

Maria never adapts to Edmonton — to the cold, the strange food, the English language she cannot seem to learn. Even the Ukrainian church across the street, a church of her religion, is strange and frightening to her; she can never pray there.

Years pass. She bears Beppi three children. The young boarders who shared her loneliness and her nostalgia leave one by one as they begin family lives of their own in Canada. Luigino is the last. When he is gone, she will have only her children to live for, and they are very Canadianized. Lella, her youngest and favourite, already makes fun of her: "Funny Mummy, you no speak too good" (p. 27).

The mood, the tone, of "The Last Young Man" is melancholy. Maria's thoughts are tinged with regret. Regret for what she has left behind. Regret that things in the present are at best only tolerable.

Maria is an outside figure. The seven-point observations made about Kroetsch's character apply also to her. She is lonely and nostalgic. She feels uprooted. Her viewpoint is different. So are her values. She cannot, for example, understand her Canadian neighbours who make love in the middle of the afternoon with the window open so that their cries can be heard from the yard and who, by the reports of her children, live on hot dogs, chips, and Cokes.

If Maria does not yet suffer an identity crisis, she will. We can picture her becoming, in time, like Assunta Barone in F.G. Paci's novel *Black Madonna*[3] or like the mother in my short story "Margherita."[4] Both are archtypes of the immigrant woman, who suffers silently, her sacrifices never fully understood or appreciated by her children. In *Black Madonna* the title suggests Stoic suffering, and in "Margherita" the mother has had a stroke and cannot speak. Readers learn of her indirectly by what her two daughters have to say.

What keeps all these characters marginal? I would suggest memory. People are the sum of their experiences. It shapes their character. It colours their viewpoint. The present is seen in the light of the past, and this light can be quite different when it has been transported across an ocean. Each culture has its own lights and colours.

The ethnic short story is replete with such characters. In Austin Clarke's "They Heard A Ringing of Bells"[5] Sagaboy tells his friends how lost he sometimes feels in the "blasted five-dollars-a-week rat-trap (he) lives in, on Spadina...." "You know something?" he says. "I have never seen *one* blasted bird in this place yet, and I now remember that, for the first time! Back home, the birds chirping nice songs and then they run off to sleep. And the trees, trees all round where we was sitting down, trees dress-up in a more greener coat o'green than this grass" (p. 86). Sagaboy is from the

West Indies where the light, the shade, the landscape have an effect on life that is different from that in Canada.

John Metcalf's narrator in "The Years in Exile"[6] is from England, and he feels the same. He is an old man, a famous Canadian writer. Sitting on the patio, he remembers with the clarity of age his boyhood in England.

> I have lived in Canada for sixty-one years covered now with honours yet in my reveries the last half century fades, the books, the marriages, the children, and the friends. I find myself dwelling more and more on my childhood years in England, the years when I was nine or ten. My mind is full of pictures (p. 206).

The story portrays an outsider haunted by memories of a past in another country. Despite a long successful career in Canada this man demonstrates a sense of loneliness, alienation and acute loss.

The title has a double edge to it. The narrator feels in exile from what? The English countryside? Or from his own past? That Metcalf, himself an English immigrant, made him a famous Canadian writer is also significant, for writers should never feel estranged from their cultural roots — that is, their raw materials.

It is for this reason that young writers usually begin by exploring their background, and many will confess to being able not to produce anything of value until they are firmly sure of their roots. Only then can they grow.

Consider the works of some major writers. Alice Munro's first story collection, *Dance of the Happy Shades*,[7] which established her reputation by winning a Governor General's Medal, draws inspiration from Ontario of the 1940's. Margaret Laurence's early collection, *Bird at the Window*[8], explores her Manitoba Scottish-Protestant background. Hugh Hood's *Flying a Red*

Kite,[9] which some critics maintain revolutionized the short story in Canada, is set principally in Montreal's English-speaking community. Margaret Atwood's *Dancing Girls*[10] is about various women dancing to someone else's tune; in other words, the collection probes the author's feminine background.

In Anne Hébert's collection, *Le Torrent*, the figure of the outsider recurs often. The contrast and conflict between the dominant society and a person from a minority group is the subject of "Un grand mariage." The Metis woman, Délia, journeys to Quebec City from the far north in pursuit of Augustin, the white man who promised to marry her. In the city she finds that Augustin has married into respectable French society. Délia spends the rest of her life in the city the victim of exploitation and sexual abuse.[11] In Hébert's other stories the marginal figures are often so extreme in their condition that they take on symbolic meaning for Quebec society.

A young Jewish woman who emigrates to Canada after escaping the Nazis is the subject of Monique Bosco's *Un amour maladroit*.[12] Rachel is a displaced person in many senses: as a war refugee, as a Jew, as an uprooted person. She is also unloved by her family, alienated from her environment, unable to belong to French society, an outsider in the world itself. Bosco herself is an immigrant to Canada and uses this outsider perspective in another work, *La Femme de Loth*,[13] Where do these people belong? Two old English ladies try to deal with this question in Henry Kreisel's story, "Two Sisters in Geneva." One sister has lived in the Canadian west for many years, the other has settled in Florence, Italy. Both consider their adopted countries home.[14]

The characters in such early collections are part of minority groups; as such, they fall easily into the outside figure category. These adults and children manifest the loneliness, sense of exile and lack of identity found in the characters from immigrant stories.

Writers of immigrant background begin the same way: by deciding who they are. This is no easy task in a mosaic society. Often the job involves looking back at one's country of origin. In the tapestry of Italo-Canadian writing, the suggestion of going back to Italy for a missing part of oneself is a recurrent motif, and has produced a multitude of marginal characters in poems, plays, stories and novels.

The four stories in Alexandre Amprimoz' collection, *In Rome*, recapture his boyhood in that city. The author writes about his younger self in the third person, as if Nestor Daimin were someone else, which in a sense he is, the author having changed so much in the intervening years. Yet the man continues to be influenced by the boy. In "Seeds for the Sonata of the Birds,"[15] for instance, the first person narrator is on a holiday in Rome and records his impressions in a diary, but he cannot do so without a flood of memories about the escapades of Nestor, his younger self.

Similarly in my short story, "Roots," Berto Donati feels that he has left a younger self behind in his native village — "a younger Berto forever in Villa" — and he knows he must go back to fetch him.[16] The story juxtaposes life in Italy with life in Canada, as if he is trying to live in both places at once, a condition not uncommon among immigrants. Like the characters in F.G. Paci's *Black Madonna* and *The Italians* Berto does not know if he is Italian or Canadian; he remains on the margins of both cultures.

But even when identity is not the principal question, characters in the ethnic short story tend to have different emotional terms of reference because of their cultural background. In "Bottled Roses" Toronto's

Darlene Madott describes how personal secrets in a family isolate its members.[17] Her characters spread over three generations of Italo-Canadians, but the observation has the ring of general truth; we all have dark corners to our minds. Madott's story, "The Namesake," demonstrates the view that "people become the name they are given, or are called after the thing their own natures have found."[18] In Morley Callaghan's classic, "A Wedding Dress," for instance, Miss Lena Schwartz becomes a victim of the label "spinster" by which others judge her.[19] Callaghan's stories of little people are moral tales reminiscent of Chekhov, Maupassant and Latin American short stories.

The question of identity is an important one in ethnic Canadian writing. Canadian expatriate writers bring an added dimension to this issue. Like Anne Hébert Mavis Gallant lived in Paris for many years and is well aware of the position of the immigrant, the foreigner, the exile. In her many stories Gallant repeatedly deals with people who are outsiders in one way or another. In "The Four Seasons" Carmela is a little Italian servant girl in an English household in Italy. Mr. and Mrs. Unwin find themselves an expatriate English couple exiled in Italy as Mussolini is about to go to war with Britain. The stories in Gallant's *From the Fifteenth District* all deal with exiles and immigrants. When these are women the marginal status is made even more extreme as it is in "The Moslem Wife."[20]

It is clear Canadian short story writers belong to international literary traditions. The literary relatives of the outsider figures in Canadian stories can be found in Maupassant, in Tolstoy's Ivan Ilyich, in Kafka and Alberto Moravia. In his *Racconti romani* Moravia has a gallery of urban exiles, men and women displaced in their own society.[21] The first to take an international approach to writing have been Canadian expatriate writers. Expatriate authors face many problems similar to those of ethnic writers. Some become cosmopolitan and draw inspiration from that experience, as does Mavis Gallant. Others look back to Canada to remember who they are, as does Mordecai Richler. One, Norman Levine, has made a career of re-establishing connections with his roots. In the stories in *Thin Ice*[22] he repeatedly travels back to Canada to fill up notebooks with his impressions.

Levine retains the viewpoint of an outsider. Part of the success of his works rests on the fact that his camera is set at a different angle.

The contact is necessary for him if he is to avoid the fate of Alexander Marsden in the story, "A Canadian Upbringing." In it, a young Levine admires the author of a book he has come across. Marsden wrote the book many years before he emigrated to England. Levine, finding himself in England, decides to look up the idol who had so influenced him as an aspiring writer, only to learn that Marsden now makes his living by constructing windmill toys. It seems that Marsden has jeopardized his career by severing his roots.

"Go back to Canada,"[23] Marsden tells Levine, and this the young author does. But not to any Canada; it is the Jewish component of the Canadian mosaic that he seeks out.

This raises some complex questions about the position of the writer in a mosaic society. If an author is the interpreter of his culture, to which culture does he belong? Does he view the experience of other groups only from the outside? Can a writer be ethnic and mainstream at the same time or is there an evolution?

Some writers try to be both. A number of stories suggest that, in fact, a cultural fragmentation does exist. In Margaret Atwood's *Dancing Girls*, for example, two selections have immigrant protagonists, and if we compare these with the rest of the book, we see that Atwood is unable to get into the mind of the Vietnamese in "The Man from Mars" and the Arab in "Dancing Girls." She tells what happens without providing insight into why.

Other writers have faced the same problem, for in a mosaic society we are all ethnics in relation to our neighbours — different in culture and therefore viewpoint. The Canadian narrator in Gwendolyn MacEwen's story, "Snow," does not understand her immigrant boyfriend's fascination with snow.[24] The Canadian narrator of Irena Friedman's "The Nielson Chocolate Factory" cannot fathom her Portuguese landlord's reason for wanting to evict her; readers can only surmise that it has something to do with pride.[25]

Invariably, such stories use the minor-character-narrator technique, but they are not as forceful. The central character remains partly hidden.

If a common denominator does exist, it is the immigrant experience — the one experience to which we can all relate; this is the glue that holds the mosaic together.

When I wrote "Details from the Canadian Mosaic"[26] I considered calling the small boy protagonist Nikos and making him Greek. I finally named him Mario, but the story would have made its points equally well had I called him Gustav, Estevan, or Sean.

It may be a truism to say that all Canadians are of immigrant descent, but it is also true that we are immigrants within our own country. A rancher from the Cariboo, a fisherman from the West Coast, and a Vancouver businessman — all are different from one another, and together these B.C. residents are different from their countrymen in the prairies or Ontario.

In Stephen Scobie's "Streak Mosaic"[27] the girlfriend — a painter from the prairies — is in Vancouver; she feels crowded by the mountains. "To her, they just filled up air. She said it was a walled city, emotionally under siege. She wanted the walls to fall down, and all that empty air to come rushing in. The city exploding to meet it" (p. 260-61).

Her boyfriend replies:

> The first twenty years of your life, you never saw a mountain. Never saw the sea. I mean, Christ, what does that *do* to people? I lived by the sea all my life. Vacations on Vancouver Island. Camped at Long Beach. I mean, what did you think about, when you read about the sea. When you were in school, reading a poem, and the poet was talking about the sea, what did you think of? What kind of image came into your mind? (p. 262)

Gwendolyn MacEwen makes the same point effectively in her fine short story, "The House of the Whale."[28] Lucas is a native Indian from the Queen Charlotte Islands. He leaves his village to work in the canneries on the mainland, and then teams up with a white friend Aaron to travel across Canada. The farther he goes, the less sure of his identity he is.

"Lucas," Aaron tells him. "I forgot to tell you something. In B.C. you were still something. Here, you won't even exist. You'll live on the sweet circumference of things, looking into the center; you'll be less than a shadow or a ghost" (p. 171).

Like Jonas, Lucas is swallowed whole by the city of Toronto, his destiny "to lose myself, to become neither Indian nor white but a kind of grey nothing, floating between two worlds" (p. 171). Ending up in jail for having killed another man in a drunken brawl, he writes a letter to his friend Aaron, telling his brief life's story and asking if the totems have all fallen in his native village. Suddenly this — knowing and remembering who he is — is the most important thing.

Writers of ethnic origin will find empathy with Lucas' confusion, nostalgia, and identity crisis. Most of them stand off center in relation to North American society. As we have seen, their search for identity has led to a number of outside figures.

Rocco Sebastiano, the grandfather, in my short story, "El Dorado,"[29] would agree with Lucas. As a young man, he was happy in his native village, where he worked as a bell-maker, until he was drafted to fight in the First World War. Afterwards, unemployed, he smuggled himself into Canada, one of the w.o.p.'s of the 1920's. Canada (or America, the two being the same for him) was the El Dorado of his youth. Arriving there, however, he suffered all the hardships common to immigrants so that in his dreams El Dorado became his native village. Like Lucas, he felt that getting back there was what really mattered.

And getting back there is exactly what most Italo-Canadian writers have done in their fiction. As Caterina Edwards put it in her subtly complex first novel, *The Lion's Mouth*, "I wrote of Venice... and I still do, not from choice but need."[30]

In the novel Bianca Bolcato makes several attempts to understand her cousin, Marco Mazzin — who is the personification of Venice — but she finds that her perception of him changes as she becomes more Canadianized. This leads her to wonder if he has really changed or if just her view of him has shifted. What is the difference between illusion and reality?

In other words, the picture changes with the light and the camera's angle.

For the writers, the journey back to Italy — to their identity — is never an easy one. They have been away, and their camera's angle has forever been altered. They saw North America with the eyes of Italians and felt not quite at home. Now, they see Italy with the eyes of Canadians, and their ambivalence — their sense of duality — remains. Like Lucas, they stay "on the sweet circumference of things, looking into the center" wherever they live.

In Caterina Edwards' story "Island of the Nightingale"[31] the young woman narrator returns to her native Trieste, but she is still an outside figure because, having lived abroad, she has different values from the more conservative local people.

Perhaps Lucas would have remained an outsider had he returned to the Queen Charlottes? Perhaps Scobie's prairie artist would have changed after she saw the mountains and the ocean? Perhaps El Dorado exists only in the memory of Rocco Sebastiano?

In Canadian writing the short story is dominated by the perspective of the outsider, the marginal figure. This is a characteristic that many Canadian stories share with the short fiction of many other countries: the *conte* of France, the *racconto* of Italy, the *novelle* of Germany and the *cuento* of Latin America. The immigrant perspective found in Italian-Canadian stories and other ethnic stories has made us aware of our literary ties with the rest of the world and has, paradoxically, focused attention on the true nature of our own culture.[32] The irony is that our multicultural society is reaching self-recognition through this process of looking out beyond our borders.[33] As we re-evaluate our immigrant roots we find that narrow nationalism and dominant mainstream culture is pushed off to the side little by little. Regional and ethnic cultures begin to assert themselves more and more. The process makes us more ethnic and at the same time more Canadian. The immigrant seems less foreign. "I am part of all that I have met," says Tennyson's Ulysses. He could have added that what he has met is now also a part of him, and his viewpoint will be forever altered by it. Ithaca will never be the same when he gets back. In part he will feel an outsider in his own city.

NOTES

1 *The Best Modern Canadian Short Stories*, ed. M. Wolfe (Edmonton: Hurtig, 1978), p. 96.

2 *The Journal of Canadian Fiction*, Vol. II, No. 2 (1973).

3 Ottawa: Oberon Press, 1981.

4 *Other Selves* (Montreal: Guernica, 1985).

5 *Toronto Short Stories*, ed. M. Wolfe and D. Daymond (Toronto: Doubleday, 1977).

6 *Canadian Short Stories, Third Series*, ed. R. Weaver (Toronto: Oxford, 1978).

7 Toronto: McGraw-Hill Ryerson, 1968.

8 Toronto: McClelland and Stewart, 1970. See the African stories in Laurence's *The Tomorrow Tamer* (Toronto: McClelland and Stewart, 1970).

9 Toronto: The Ryerson Press, 1962.

10 Toronto: McClelland and Stewart, 1978.

11 *Le Torrent* (Montreal: Editions HMH, 1976) pp. 149-50.

12 *Un amour maladroit* (Paris: Gallimard, 1961).

13 *La Femme de Loth* (Montreal: HMH, 1970). Bosco's works are novels but the examples could be stories by Jacques Ferron, Yves Thériault, Claire Martin or Roch Carrier.

14 *The Almost Meeting and Other Stories* (Edmonton: NeWest Press, 1983), pp. 130-32.

15 *In Rome*, (Toronto: Three Trees Press, 1980), p. 19.

16 *The Journal of Canadian Fiction*, Vol. III, No. 2 (1974).

17 *Aurora*, ed. M. Wolfe (Toronto: Doubleday, 1978).

18 *Canadian Fiction Studies*, Vol. XIV, No. 1 (1982), p. 117.

19 *Toronto Short Stories, op. cit.*

20 Toronto: Macmillan of Canada, 1973.

21 Milano: Bompiani, 1954.

22 Ottawa: Deaneau and Greenberg, 1981.

23 *The Best Modern Canadian Short Stories, op. cit.*

24 *Sunlight and Shadows*, eds. J.A. McNeill and G.A. Sorestead (Toronto: Thomas Nelson, 1974).

25 *Toronto Short Stories, op. cit.*

26 *Other Selves* (Montreal: Guernica, 1985).

27 *Horizon* (1979).

28 *Toronto Short Stories, op. cit.*

29 *Queen's Quarterly*, Vol. 89, No. 4, (1982).

30 *The Lion's Mouth* (Edmonton: NeWest Press, 1982), p. 152.

31 *Italian-Canadian Voices*, ed. C.M. Di Giovanni (Oakville: Mosaic Press, 1984.)

32 Robert Kroetsch, "Beyond Nationalism: A Prologue," *Mosaic*, XIV, 2 (1981).

33 More work needs to be done in Comparative Canadian Literature. Not only are there parallels between English and French Canadian writing but also similarities with Latin American writing. Jack Hodgins and Madeleine Ferron share their magic realism with Machado de Assis, Carlos Fuentes, Mario Vargas Llosa.

ROBERTA SCIFF-ZAMARO

Black Madonna: A Search for the Great Mother

English writing in Canada has a relatively short tradition and thus it has been difficult to examine ancient mythic patterns. Instead Canadian literary criticism has been concerned with an environmentalist interpretation of our literature since themes of nature can easily be traced to experiences of the frontier and settlement.[1] The literary traditions that later immigrants brought to Canada do not have roots in the frontier or the homestead but in the old countries. Italian-Canadian writers demonstrate the identifiable influences of Italian cultural traditions. In his novels, *The Italians, Black Madonna* and *The Father* Frank Paci has turned to the old family myths and beliefs of the Mediterrenean.

The complex cluster of meanings associated with the Italian *mamma* has been demonstrated in countless works of literature, painting, music, opera and folk songs. From the thousands of Madonnas in parish churches to the old Alpine song *Oi cara mamma* to the various popular songs dedicated to the figure of the mamma, it is clear that this image is deeply ingrained in the Italian psychology. In *Black Madonna* Paci has employed the figure of the mamma not only to examine the power of this image in his family oriented immigrant community but also to explore the universal dimensions of the Canadian novel.

Frank Paci's *Black Madonna* is the story of the Baroni, a family of Italian immigrants in Canada.[2] The novel opens with an event that is crucial for the future development of the narrative, the day of Adamo Baroni's funeral. Adamo, the father, had left the small village in the Abruzzi where he had grown up to move to "America" hoping for a better life. Settling in Sault Ste. Marie, a town in Northern Ontario, he had spent his whole life working to provide for his children all the things he had missed during his childhood and adolescence. Assunta, the mother, had moved to Canada from her village in the Marche to marry Adamo, a man she actually did not know since, in a sense, their marriage had been by proxy. At the opening of the novel Marie, the eldest daughter, has already left home and moved to Toronto to receive the longed-for education. Her brother, Joey, still lives in his parent's house and works in the steel plant where his father had spent most of his life. Although the novel deals with a typical family of Italian immigrants, to define it merely as a portrait of "the immigrant experience," however, would be to reduce its import. *Black Madonna*, in fact, must not be read as the synthesis of the events in the life of an Italian family adjusting to Canada but, rather, as a quest for identity out of a split self which sees the two children as protagonists. Such a quest gives rise to deep problems of communication between the parents and their children, between the "older generation" and the "younger generation," which could lead to a total lack of understanding.

The story itself develops around two nuclei which are in turn represented by the Adamo-Joey and the Assunta-Marie relationships. Our analysis will concentrate on the latter, and it is in such a context that we would propose two levels of reading. On the one hand the story can be simply viewed as the portrait of the two main characters, Assunta and Marie, and of the difficulties the former encounters in adapting to a new country and the latter in accepting her Italian origins. Moreover, it is also the portrait of the lack of understanding between the two women which will eventually lead to a complete break, and of the daughter's quest for her real hidden self. Marie's quest could be represented as a process of self-knowledge characterized by the two phases of rejection/acceptance of her mother and, implicity, or herself as well. On the other hand we can discern a mythological sub-code which suggests a second level of reading of the novel according to which Marie's quest involves a search for the Great Mother, the female principle, which has been subverted with the advent of patriarchal society.

The relationship between Assunta and Marie has always been problematic. It is especially through the extensive flash-backs leading us through Marie's childhood and adolescence that we acquire an understanding of the reasons for why the difficulties between the two women had arisen. Marie's behaviour toward her family has always been a negative one; she is portrayed as "rather aloof and distant, giving... the impression she was too good for the family" (p. 5). At her father's funeral she appears so changed that it is hard even for her own brother to identify her with the girl he used to know as his sister. She has left her family, has attended university as she had been determined to do since her childhood and, moreover, has married an English Canadian in a Protestant church. All these steps have been detrimental to her relationship with Assunta, a relationship which had always been quite strained and which, as the years went by, had deteriorated more and more. To Marie her mother is nothing but a stranger, a being beyond her own reach. It is with deep hardness that she overstresses such a fact when Joey hints to her that it is their duty, now that their father is dead, to look after Assunta:

> How can she be my mother if she's never had the slightest idea of who I was? ... We've never spoken the same language even. How can she be my mother? She's never had the

least comprehension of what I was doing in school or what I wanted in life. All she did was cook and wash for me. And hit me a lot when I was a kid. There are no two people so different as we are. She's like a fossil. She's in the wrong time and the wrong country. So how can she be my mother? Tell me (p. 17).

Already when still an adolescent, Marie had felt that she did not really belong to her family, she had been almost ashamed of it. The relationship with her brother had always been somehow superficial since she had a superiority complex. With her father she had never encountered a real problem; although he did not meet her canons, he at least did not bother her. Thus the actual obstacle had been represented by her mother.

The first problem was Assunta's coarseness, her lack of refinement, but more than that it was Assunta's behaviour, her failing in not respecting Marie as a person, her way of imposing her own will. In such a difficult period as the adolescence could be, Marie, while discovering her own femininity, was inclined to exaggerate some defects, first of all her weight. Especially in this respect, she would feel that her mother was unable to understand her since her fatness was actually Assunta's fault. The latter was seen as a tyrant when food was concerned; every meal developed into a drama, a tug-of-war between daughter and mother, Marie trying to limit her eating, Assunta seeing in such a behaviour a personal affront to which she would react by imposing herself with deeper stubbornness. Moreover, for Marie it was a dishonour that "her mother was an illiterate peasant. And even worse — a mail-order bride" (p. 37), that Assunta had not been able or, perhaps, had been unwilling to adapt to the new country, persisting in certain despicable habits she had brought with her from Italy as, for instance, the habit of keeping a chamber-pot under her bed. All this made it hard for Marie to identify herself as the daughter, the offspring, of such a disagreeable being. To make these feelings even worse there was also the almost complete lack of communication between them; Assunta did not even speak English and thus she had failed to be that confidant her daughter was in need of. Marie's resentment toward her family also infected the outer world, the Italian community she belonged to. The shame she felt for her Italian origins had become deeper and deeper; the environment in which she had grown up had become more and more unbearable; everything was revolting, the women, the children, the houses themselves. Marie's adolescence could be summarized in a few words, lack of communication, isolation, humiliations. At last, she was offered a chance to break away from such an environment by being accepted by the University of Toronto, an event which led to the complete break with her mother.

If Marie's psychology is clearly portrayed in the novel, Assunta instead appears as its most enigmatic character who, however, must not be dismissed before a closer analysis. Adamo's death appears to be decisive for the following development of the story since it affects Assunta so strongly as to take away from her any desire to keep on living. The title itself, *Black Madonna*, refers to this figure of a woman who, at her husband's death, decides to wear the deepest mourning, thus following one of the fundamental dictates of the culture she belongs to. The first instance of how deeply certain customs are rooted in the first generation of Italians in Canada is given by the scene in which Assunta and the other "black madonnas" of the neighbourhood are keeping vigil by the bedside of the dead Adamo. Such a custom is perpetuated in most parts of Italy, it belongs to its culture, and failing to follow it would imply a break-away from the laws of one's own land. This is unthinkable in Assunta's case especially when we recognize that her failure in adapting to the new world is mainly due to the fact that the culture brought over from the old country is too strong to be effaced by a new environment. It is easy to understand that to Marie such a custom appears as a "masquerade," which implies the lack of any inner, significant value, since her education differs from her mother's. To understand Assunta's behaviour would mean to understand a culture alien to Marie. At the same time, however, the ancient ritual that to Marie does not represent anything else but another example of her mother's primitiveness, of her ignorance, actually demonstrates how strong is the hold of her cultural traditions even when unrooted from their land.

Assunta appears as the typical Italian woman of the first generation of immigrants; strict, lacking any understanding of her own children, attached to primitive rituals which are out of place in the new world, the land of progress, and who shows no will whatsoever to adapt to the new country. This, however, is just one side of the coin; Assunta appears to be characterized by a two-fold nature. Her first side is so strong that quite often it overshadows the underlying, true nature which, however, begins to reveal itself little by little. This puzzling figure rises as the symbol for a whole generation of women completely alienated from the Canadian society in which they happen to be living. These women too often have been misunderstood and discarded as anachronistic, but the understanding of Assunta's motives would help in a better appreciation of them as well; it would lead to the reshuffling of certain beliefs or, better, prejudices, and to the recognition of their active role in the building of the new world.

To Assunta her coming to Canada had meant to accept a life of exile in which her roles of wife and mother become the most prominent features. These are roles imposed on her by destiny, and it is by fulfilling such duties that she tries to create a balance in her new life. To attain such a balance she tries to create a world based on a compromise between her former life and the new one, namely to live in a foreign country but maintaining at the same time her mother tongue as well as the culture and traditions of the old country. Perhaps, it is not so easy to understand how she could be so obstinate in not trying to adapt to the new world, but there are strong reasons to justify such behaviour. In the first place her coming to Canada had not been for Assunta a completely free choice but, rather, a must since, having already passed the marriageable age, she did not feel able to reject what could have been her last chance to get married. Moreover, to look after a family in a foreign country and to try to do it in the best possible way had already been a hard task for her. Assunta probably had neither the time, the energy nor the courage to undergo a process of assimilation to the new culture especially if we take into account the fact that the social facilities apt to meet the needs of newcomers were almost non-existent at that time. Viewed in this light, it becomes clear that to be the perfect housewife had been a way to give a sense to her new existence, and even her obsession with food becomes more understandable. Food has always had an important place in the Italian culture; every meal represents almost a ritual that few women, and especially women like Assunta, would fail to perform. Moreover, when we take into account that in most of the cases moving to the new world had been due to extreme poverty — the way Assunta appears in an old picture "extreme thinness and... particular angularity of her face" (p. 64) is a proof of this fact — the psychological reasons for her way of behaving become evident. It appears obvious that when she was living in Italy she was not nourished particularly well, and it is also clear that to make sure that her children have everything she had missed is of utmost importance. Spending her life in the kitchen and seeing her children grow strong and healthy represents for Assunta a deep satisfaction, a victory over all the privations of her past.

All these aspects of Assunta's nature have to be put together bit by bit by the reader, since she is presented as a highly puzzling character whose thoughts are ungraspable. There is however a scene in the novel which is quite relevant for a full understanding of this woman, the scene in which Joey goes to Padre Sarlo, the priest of the Italian church, to ask him advice since he is more and more frightened by his mother's behaviour after Adamo's death. It is Padre Sarlo who begins to disclose the unknown side of Assunta's personality. From him Joey discovers that his mother lights a candle for the husband every day, a fact which astonishes him since it is not in tune with his belief that his parents did not care at all for one another. Joey realizes that the lack of open manifestations of affection between the parents was not due to a lack of love but merely to a certain kind of education. He also realizes that Assunta's behaviour after her husband's death is the result of particular customs of her upbringing. Customs which will probably appear as cruel, barbaric and absurd to a stranger, but which are so deeply rooted in the culture of a certain community that none of its members would have ever dared to violate them.

Padre Sarlo summarizes the life of these Italian immigrants who had left their own country to ensure a better life for their children; who had spent their whole existences working and, at the end, had to witness something extremely painful. Their own children began to part from their families, their culture, their origins, to the point of becoming strangers to their own parents thus taking all value away from a life of sacrifices.

Padre Sarlo in a sense seems to act as a mouthpiece directed at the new generation of Italian-Canadians, in the effort to clarity the many sides of the prismatic nature of the old generation. A nature which is unknown and ungraspable for the very reason that the old generation failed to find the right words to make itself understood since there was a gap between parents and children, a gap due to the use of a different language, both in a literal and metaphoric sense. Thus if ever Assunta had failed to be a good mother, her failure could be justified by the fact that such a task would have been hard for anyone in a foreign country; a country where one's own children must find an identity to overcome the duality in which they have been born and brought up: conflict between family and outer society. The message is clear; only by coming to terms with its own origins and accepting them, will the new Italian-Canadian generation, symbolized in the novel by Marie and Joey, be able to find an identity which will allow it to feel that it really belongs in the country of its birth. An identity which, however, will be characterized by a full consciousness of its own roots and its own cultural background. The duality of Italian and Canadian will thus be overcome, giving life to a new identity symbolized by the term *Italo-Canadian* in which both components are present not in tension but in symbiosis.

It is in Marie's quest to find her true self out of a split identity that the archetype of the Great Mother emerges investing the quest with a mythological dimension. When mentioning the archetype of the Great Mother we are referring to the primordial feminine principle present in the collective unconscious. As Erich Neumann observes in his *The Great Mother*, the female principle appears to have a double nature; on the one hand it is inherent in the psyche itself, on the other hand it manifests itself through the projections of images or symbols:

When analytical psychology speaks of the primordial image or archetype of the Great Mother, it is referring, not to any concrete image existing in space and time, but to an inward image at work in the human psyche. The symbolic expression of this psychic phenomenon is to be found in the figures of the Great Goddess represented in the myths and artistic creations of mankind.

The effects of this archetype may be followed through the whole of history, for we can demonstrate its workings in the rites, myths, symbols, of early man and also in the dreams, fantasies, and creative works of the sound as well as the sick man of our own day.[2]

The fact that *Black Madonna* represents a projection of the archetype of the Great Mother is already hinted by the title itself. On a literal level, Assunta becomes the ''black madonna'' because of the mourning after her husband's death; such a connotation, however, has a far-reaching effect when we deal on a symbolic level. As again Erich Neumann points out:

The term Great Mother, as a partial aspect of the Archetypal Feminine, is a late abstraction, presupposing a highly developed speculative consciousness. And indeed, it is only relatively late in the history of mankind that we find the Archetypal Feminine designated as Magna Mater. But it was worshipped and portrayed many thousands of years before the appearance of the term.[3]

Thus the figure of the Great Mother, or Great Goddess, happens to have been extensively worshipped much earlier than the coinage of the term itself. As Robert Graves observes in his *The White Goddess*, at first the Great Goddess was the only power to be worshipped but later on, with the advent of the institution of monogamy, her role became less influential and she was reduced to consort of the Father-God.[4] The most striking change took place, however, in the Judaic and Christian societies as well as, generally speaking, in every society based on patriarchy. In the Christian mythology we can observe a radical subversion of the Great Goddess myth. It would be proper, in fact, to point out at this stage that the figure of the Great Mother has a three-fold nature; in her first manifestation she presents herself as the white goddess of birth and growth; in her second one, as the red goddess of battle and love; in her third one, as the black goddess of death and divination. In Christian mythology the triple Goddess is almost completely effaced as such, and it is substituted by a God, triple in nature himself. Her figure, however, is still present in Christian mythology in the person of Mary, purged of course of any connotation referring to her original status, who is relegated to the role of Mother of God. Anyhow, her very name is a reminiscence of an ancient sea-goddess who was nothing else but the Great Goddess herself under a different form. As again Graves in fact points out, "[the] charming Virgin with the blue robe and pearl necklace was the ancient pagan Sea-goddess Marian in transparent disguise — Marian, Miriam, Marianne (*Sea Lamb*) Myrrhine, Myrtea, Myrrha, Maria or Marina, patroness of poets and lovers and proud mother of the Archer of Love."[5] When we identify in Mary, mother of God, the figure of the Great Mother, the connection between the latter and the "black madonna" is clear if we think that in Italian Madonna is another name used to define the Mother of God. Moreover, it would not be out of place to notice here that the statue of the Virgin in procession, referred to in the novel in relation to Marie's past, recalls Grave's sea-goddess in disguise: "The bier holding the large statue of Our Lady of Mount Carmel... Our Lady in powder-blue and white holding a scapular medal in her outstreched hand, and dollar bills pasted like wreaths around her neck" (p. 25).

Returning to the figure of the "black madonna," also her attribute of "black" is another hint at the Great

Mother and, more precisely, of her black phase, the Hecate phase, connected with death and the underworld and again referred to by Graves as the Black Goddess, or Goddess of Wisdom, mysterious sister of the White one. In this context the critic makes an interesting reference to the Sicilian "black virgins," term which could easily be replaced by "black madonnas," since in the Christian tradition madonna implies virgin, and so called "because they derive from an ancient tradition of Wisdom as Blackness."[6] In our novel the black madonna is represented by Assunta, the mysterious, almost sibylline character who appears to her daughter as a monster. In her quest for an identity, Marie constantly finds an obstacle in the overpowering figure of her mother. During her childhood, the mother appears as an actual tyrant who has imprisoned Marie on two levels, a physical one represented by her fatness, and a psychological one, represented by the Italian environment she feels as alien. During her maturity, Assunta turns into a ghost haunting her mind.

The image of the mother turned into a phantom of her daughter's mind reappears in different Canadian novels by women writers; in each case this image always represents the projection of the black goddess entrapped inside and who needs to be released to reach an identity. If we consider for a moment Margaret Atwood's *Lady Oracle*, we see that Joan, the heroine, is portrayed as searching for her real self, and throughout the quest is constantly haunted by the figure of her mother who is again represented as a tyrant during Joan's childhood, and as a phantom of her psyche in her adulthood.[7] Although Joan has succeeded in freeing herself from her mother's influence in a physical sense, namely by getting rid of her fatness and by moving to a complete new life, her mother, nevertheless, has become an obsession on a psychological level. She has turned into a projection of Joan's fears to become a reflection of her own mother. At first glance Joan does not realize that she cannot reject the figure of her mother since the latter is part of her own self, which again refers to the archetype Great Mother. Once the Goddess lost most of her power and was reduced to Father-God's consort, the daughters she had from him were "limited versions of herself — herself in various young-moon and full-moon aspects."[8] Although her body has been rescued from the black goddess, her psyche is still her prisoner a fact which is perceived by Joan during her experiments of automatic writing. The words she ends up with, always refer to the same image of woman living "under the earth somewhere, or inside something, a cave or a huge building... She was enormously powerful, almost like a goddess, but it was an unhappy power" (p. 224). Such a woman is Joan's mother as well as a reflection of Joan herself. She is felt to be powerful almost like a goddess, the black goddess dwelling in the underworld; she is perceived as living in a huge building, namely Joan's former body, and she still is an unhappy power because not in harmony with the other two phases of the trinity, the white goddess and the red goddess.

Moving to another Canadian novel, Anne Hébert's *Kamouraska*, we notice that its heroine, Elisabeth, is involved in a search for identity which again refers to the same archetype.[9] The search always takes place in a state of drowsiness, and in all her visions Elisabeth always sees her mother standing beside her. Even though such a figure is not so obsessive as that of Joan's mother, it nevertheless presents many characteristics of the black goddess. She is described as always wearing black robes, *costumée en grand-mère* (p. 52) even when she was only seventeen and, moreover, as trying to foretell the future. Elisabeth herself is portrayed as a projection of the black goddess she has inside and who she must release in order to discover her true identity and start a new life.

The same pattern followed by Joan in *Lady Oracle* to free herself reappears in *Black Madonna*. Although in due time Marie is able to free herself in a literal sense by getting away from her family, and especially from her mother's influence, to begin a new life by herself, the attained freedom turns out to be an incomplete one. As soon as she moves to Toronto, Marie begins to undergo a process of metamorphosis which is intended to efface anything which links her to her past and in particular to her mother. The first step toward her new identity is to get rid of her fatness, imposed on her by Assunta, which implies the rejection of food. "Since her first year at university she had stopped eating Italian food altogether. Later it wasn't only Italian food, but anything having to do with her mother's dishes." (p. 100) The rejection of food symbolizes the rejection of the mother herself, who has always been associated first of all with eating. From this process of metamorphosis Marie comes out completely changed; she is a new person with no links with her Italian origins: "She had shed her odious cocoon, looked bone-thin and gloriously herself" (p. 97). The break is not only represented in her physical appearance but also in the fact that she choses a different kind of life; she decides to be a "woman professor," and not the traditional wife and mother she was supposed to become according to Assunta's canons. Although she is able to free herself in a physical sense, her mother continues to pursue her and turns into an obsession. At the very moment Marie is completely sure to have disentangled herself from Assunta, the latter begins to appear to her under the form of hallucinations. The first instance of Assunta's return is offered by the scene in which Marie is victim of a presumed swoon during which everything she has been trying to reject for so long imposes on her with utmost strength. In her vision, Marie sees her mother's Christmas table regally set out; she is attracted towards it as if towards a magnet, and from it she derives an inexplicable pleasure. Since the scene mentioned has a highly sexual import, its meaning is far-reaching. On a rational level Marie has refused everything connected with her origins, but in her unconscious the food, which does not represent anything but a symbol of her mother and, therefore, of her own nature as well, turns out to be a fundamental part of her own self; it is something she really needs and desires, and from which she feels highly rewarded. All the marks of her origins that she has tried to efface for so long have overcome her in a moment of weakness. Moreover, since the *vision* has strong sexual connotations, it also means that in the moment when her subconscious, her true inner self, gains an advantage over her, she is led to give vent to her sensuality, her womanhood, which she has tried to suffocate since her adolescence as something too primitive, too Italian. Later on Marie actually feels her mother's presence: "At that moment Marie felt the unmistakable presence of her mother's dark thin figure in the room. ... [Marie] got up and looked at herself in the mirror. Her face was old and ravaged. It was as if her mother were staring back at her" (pp. 116-117). As we have already noticed in regard to Joan's case: in these moments Marie just begins to realize that she cannot reject the figure of her mother since the latter is part of herself. What is fighting in her is the Hecate figure, the black goddess, but she is unable to accept it since she still does not have a full perception of it. As a matter of fact, Marie realizes that "there was something wrong with her. She could feel it in her bones — something so deep and so much a part of her she couldn't bring it to the surface" (p. 115). What her hallucinations suggest is that although she has been physically freed from Hecate, her mind is still entrapped by it. The Hecate phase, being just part of a whole, represents a positive power when in harmony with the other two phases, which in Marie's case are, however, still trapped inside the black goddess.

The white goddess of the first phase, elsewhere called Diana, of Marie's childhood and adolescence, is portrayed as imprisoned by Hecate, the symbol of the fat body from which she will eventually burst out completely new. With her new life the phase of the red goddess, of Venus, begins; a phase characterized by sexual and maternal love. Her Venus phase is symbolized by her relationship with Richard, their marriage and the birth of their son. What in a first moment appears as a new life in due time turns out to be a new battlefield, which is not out of place when we think that Venus is also the goddess of battle. Although in her Venus phase, she is still victim of the Hecate figure. It is especially in Marie's relationship with her son that such a figure imposes itself once more. As Assunta had been unable to accept the individuality of her daughter, in the same way it is very hard for Marie to accept the fact that her son is a human being completely different from her. What happens is paradoxical; for years Marie has been trying to efface any mark which could reveal her Italian origins and in so doing she has broken away more and more from her family and especially from her mother who is her most hated person, perhaps because the very symbol of such origins. From her metamorphosis she turns out completely different from the adolescent Marie but, astonishingly, she also turns out to look exactly like her mother, to the point that after Assunta's death the latter seems to come again to life in Marie's person. Such a fact deeply affects her brother Joey. She appears to him like a stranger: ''She walked over to the TV room unsteadily, opened the set and unthinkingly plopped herself onto Assunta's place at the end of the sofa. ... He watched her silently. Her black dress. Her thin shrunken frame. Her lost eyes. And was confused for a moment'' (p. 181). Although Marie has tried very hard to find a new identity by freeing herself from her mother, her attempts prove to be a complete failure since what she has not realized is that she cannot get rid of her mother, and of her past, since her mother is a projection of her own self. After all, both turn out to be "black madonnas," or rather they are the same "black madonna", since both their names refer to the same figure; Assunta and Marie are in fact both attributes of the same madonna.

Notwithstanding all her previous failures, after Assunta's death Marie is finally able to realize what is trapped inside her, thus finding her own identity. In this respect the Hope Chest functions as a wonderful symbol. Ever since her childhood Marie has been trying to open her mother's Hope Chest, a chest the latter had brought over with her from Italy and which contains family belongings. A chest which, moreover, represents a strong maternal bond since it has been handed down from mother to daughter for generations and generations. For Marie the chest has become part of a ritual; it has always attracted her as something mysterious and her curiosity to discover Assunta's hidden secrets has become stronger and stronger, but she has always been unable to find the key to open it. Her failure in finding the key symbolizes her failure in finding a key to enter and understand her mother's nature. At Assunta's death, however, Marie makes an astonishing discovery; the chest is not locked at all, and it probably has been open for a long time. Now the moment to take hold of Assunta's treasures has arrived; Marie is now ready to begin the journey into her mother's secret world. In the chest there are not such treasures as she has been cherishing for so long but just old, simple things. The chest appears to contain different layers, from more recent to older things:

> There was an assortment of bed linen and clothes immediately underneath. Pillow cases with ornate embroidery. A few towels. Some very simple cotton dresses. Common-sense underclothes of various patterns and fabrics. These seemed to have been mended recently. Underneath these was a simple black mourning dress of coarse black cotton with a kerchief and stockings. Marie noticed that as she dug deeper the contents appeared to be older, as if she were unearthing various layers of a person's life. (p. 190)

Passing from one layer to the other is like going deeper and deeper into the past; it is a retracing back her maternal lineage, a lineage lost in the mists of time. The black dress seems made exactly for her and so dressed, a black madonna of wisdom, she sets up an altar in front of the mirror. The altar is made with what she has found at the bottom of the chest, two candles and a three-folded shrine; on one side there is the picture of a young girl, on the other that of an old woman in black, and in the middle a glass casket enclosing the body of a young girl dressed in white. As Marie herself notices, "her young virginal face was so composed that Marie thought she was only sleeping" (p. 191), an image which could symbolize the positive power, the white goddess, Marie has to recover to find an identity. To come to terms with her real self Marie must go through the glass. Only by accepting her real nature, only by not rejecting her mother and her own origins, will she find her own positive identity. Assunta will continue to be a negative power until Marie will be able to release her mother, the black madonna/black goddess, from her own deeper self through the acceptance of this side of her personality. Only by accepting the black goddess inside her as part of her full self, will this goddess turn from ominous into positive power. To free herself, Marie has to descend into the maze of her psyche which, as Gilbert and Gubar point out in their *The Madwoman in the Attic*, symbolizes the descent into the cave where the Sibyl, the primordial prophetess and another extension of the Hecate figure, gives her oracles.[10]

As in the case of the archetype of the Great Mother, the cave motif is also present in *Lady Oracle* and *Kamouraska*. To free themselves, Joan and Elisabeth must descend to the Sibyl's cave which in the former's case is represented by her entering the maze of her own mind through the experiments of automatic writing, whereas in the latter's case it is expressed by the heroine's descent into the maze of her mind through those visions which take place in a state between dream and reality. Putting into order the scattered words and the scattered images they end up with from their journeys, both heroines will be able to acquire a sense of their true selves. Through a long and difficult work of interpretation and revision the meaning of such words and images will be disclosed and the original female power reconquered. In *Black Madonna*, Marie's journey into her mind takes place during the kind of trance she falls into in front of the looking-glass, which represents a shield between Marie and her own self; a mirror she has to go through and which leads again to the same figure, her mother:

> Shutting off the light she sat on the edge of the bed and looked into the mirror... She lost track of time as she sat transfixed in front of the shrine. Every so often she caught her own expression in the mirror. It was slightly perplexed. Slightly awed... Sometime later she felt her mother's presence in the room. She seemed to be lying on the bed behind her... Marie stared harder into the mirror, trying to make out the expression on her mother's face. But she was too far away. She had to peer closer. The face came closer. It was hard like a statue. She saw the thin curve of the mouth. The

sharp angular features. The deep-set eyes. "Mamma, I'm sorry," she said out loud. She waited patiently. Any answer, even no answer, would be all right... The statued hardness of her mother's face softened. Colour was restored to the bony cheeks. The face twitched with life. The corners of her mouth slowly turned upward (pp. 191-92).

The message Maries gets is a message of peace and acceptance. At last she has been able to make peace with Assunta, her self, her past; she has been able to recover her mother and origins as positive powers. Through such a recovery and acceptance she succeeds at last in finding her own identity; entering her mind, that is, she recovers her mother, her mother-land, her mother goddess, her Great Mother.

Marie is now ready to take that trip to Italy Assunta had always longed for, but had never been able to take. A trip which on the one hand is an actual trip, a last homage to a woman who had left her own country embarking on an adventure perhaps beyond herself, and which on the other hand will be a journey to her mother-land invested with a symbolical import, "It will be a strange trip" (p. 198), as Marie herself realizes.

NOTES

1 The mythic readings of George Woodcock, *Odysseus Ever Returning: Essays on Canadian Writers and Their Writings* (Toronto: McClelland and Stewart, 1970) can be contrasted to the thematic studies of Laurie Ricou, *Vertical Man/Horizontal World: Man and Landscape in Canadian Prairie Fiction* (Vancouver: University of British Columbia Press, 1973) and Clément Moisan, *La Poésie des frontières: Etude comparée des poésies canadienne et québécoise* (LaSalle: Hurtubise HMH, 1979).

2 F.G. Paci, *Black Madonna* (Ottawa: Oberon Press, 1982). All further references to this work appear in the text.

3 Erich Neumann, *The Great Mother: An Analysis of an Archetype* (New York: Bollingen, 1955), p. 3.

4 Neumann, p. 11.

5 Robert Graves, *The White Goddess* (New York: Farrar, Straus & Giroux, 1966), p. 389.

6 Graves, pp. 394-395.

7 Robert Graves, *Mammon and the Black Goddess* (New York: Doubleday, 1965), p. 162.

8 Margaret Atwood, *Lady Oracle* (Toronto: McClelland & Stewart, 1976). All further references to this work appear in the text.

9 Graves, *The White Goddess*, p. 389.

10 Anne Hébert, *Kamouraska* (Paris: Editions du Seuil, 1970). All further references to this work appear in the text.

11 Sandra Gilbert and Susan Gubar, *The Madwoman in the Attic* (New Haven, and London: Yale University Press, 1979), p. 96.

ALEXANDRE L. AMPRIMOZ and SANTE A. VISELLI

Death Between Two Cultures: Italian-Canadian Poetry

In many of the remote villages in the Italian hills it has been a custom to treat the departure of an emigrant in the same way as a death in the community. The funeral rites are performed for both the emigrant and the departed since both cease to be part of the village. It is little wonder then that this experience of death should recur often in the writing of Italian-Canadian immigrants. F.G. Paci's novel, *Black Madonna*, begins with a funeral and death and burial are prominent features in Maria Ardizzi's *Made in Italy* and *Il sapore agro della mia terra*. It is in the poetry, however, that the image of death becomes overwhelming. Saro D'Agostino's "Wake" epitomizes the experience:

> *I have been taught*
> *death is the mother of beauty, but*
> *my family takes death less seriously.*

> * * * *

> *In the living room the women have begun*
> *to wail and scream as though possessed*
> *by demons or death itself. Later on,*
> *in the middle of the night, it will*
> *become a chanting.*

> * * * *

> *The women will cry until the chant*
> *is broken and one of them collapses.*
> *Then some of the men will enter*
> *and try to help them, but the cries*
> *and chants soon begin again.*[1]

This poem implies that the literariness of the verses meet the literariness of the funeral chant. The social context may produce an analogous manner of looking at experience since the most distinctive ethnic characteristics are revealed at funerals. On a symbolic level the funeral captures the state of the immigrant in North American society. On the one hand the immigrant is the lost son of his home village, on the other he does not fully exist in the new society.

The stereotyped image of Italians in both English and French-Canadian writing is grotesque in its distortion of reality. Up to now it has affected the reading and evaluation of Italian-Canadian works. In contrast to the image of the Italian labourer with a *joie de vivre* or the happy mamma making spaghetti sauce, we find instead, a profound sense of the death experience in the poetry. Our reading of the work of Pier Giorgio Di Cicco, Len Gasparini, Mary Melfi, Fulvio Caccia, Mary di Michele, Marco Fraticelli and Antonio D'Alfonso will serve to correct this stereotype and the resulting imbalance. Our analysis of this ethnic poetry will focus on the discourse among Italian-Canadian writers, a discourse which is carried on across three languages: English, French and Italian.

From descriptions of funeral rites to symbolic and cultural death we can see that the new generation of Italian-Canadian poets has a significant influence on the development of Canadian Literature. In fact many young Canadian poets find themselves in this space of death. Their works demonstrate that these poets feel the force of a double presence: that of their own generation and that of their ethnic group. Whether by coincidence or by its dynamism Italian-Canadian writing is gradually moving from a marginal position to a more central one. One of the poets who has contributed to this recognition of Italian-Canadian writing is Pier Giorgio Di

Cicco who has been widely published in literary magazines and has produced eleven collections of poems since 1975. It was Di Cicco who encouraged other Italian-Canadian poets by editing the anthology, *Roman Candles*, and in turn has received recognition by being included in major national anthologies such as Margaret Atwood's *The New Oxford Book of Canadian Verse*. In William Toye's *The Oxford Companion to Canadian Literature* (1983) Di Cicco's writing is summarized in two articles. Despite this acceptance of Di Cicco into the mainstream of English Canadian writing, he remains very much an artist with strong roots in his background.

In an early review of Italian-Canadian writing Joseph Pivato pointed out that, "At times poems seem to be addressed as much to the dead as to the living. The elegy or elegaic elements are often used by these writers."[2] Di Cicco's "The Man Called Beppino" is a poem devoted to his dead father, a man whose presence seems to haunt much of the verse in *The Tough Romance*:

> *The man who lost his barbershop during the war,*
> *loves great white roses at the back of a house beside*
> *a highway. The roses dream with him,*
> *of being understood in clear english, or of a large*
> *Italian sun, or of walking forever on a*
> *Sunday afternoon.*[3]

The father finally dies physically in North America, however, he had died spiritually when he had to leave Arezzo. In the New World he is a lost soul, silent because of the unfamiliar language, a mere shadow of a former self, emaciated with sickness. The elegy is addressed as much to the immigrant spirits as to the reader. In the work of ethnic writers the spirits are always present and are part of the discourse. This is forcefully illustrated by Di Cicco's "Donna italiana":

> *There is the*
> *song of three thousand years, of little old men with the*
> *eyes of saints, they walk on the hillsides*
> *in the mid-day heat,*
> *ghosts, wishing me well. They are my grandfathers,*
> *and my great-grandfathers,*
>
> *and the ancient men that kept my ribs burning at*
> *Monte Cassino, in the*
> *air above my brother's corpse,*
> *in the shelled house in Arezzo, in*
>
> *Rimini, where I sat spread-eagled on the sand;*
> *they kept the ribs*
> *burning through the cold Montreal nights, and in*
> *Baltimore, behind the*
> *cold hospital where my father died. The ribs*
> *burned all the nights of my*
> *life, my gentle men, my grandfathers, ghosts in the*
> *hills...*[4]

The ribs of this poet did not stop burning when the
focus of his work moved from ancient Italian ancestors
to contemporary issues. *Flying Deeper into the Century*
is haunted by the spectre of death in many poems:
"Armageddon," "Hatching," "Things That Don't
Die," and "Asleep in the World." Near the end of the
collection the poet confesses in "Such Days":

> *I think I have been thinking of*
> *Death too much, and the green fields have been*
> *talking*
> *to me, and I've stopped up my ears with a drop of*
> *blood...*[5]

The sunny hillsides of Etruscan grandfathers have

become the green fields of the graveyard. The ancient Italian preoccupation with death, as well as personal family experiences have influenced Di Cicco's meditations on death, death in the modern century.

This concern with life and death in the Canadian city is part of the dialogue of Italian-Canadian writers. Len Gasparini, a well-established poet since the 1960's has dedicated "Il sangue" to Pier Giorgio Di Cicco. The poem is an apostrophe that is at once hyperbolic and inchoative. There is no breaking off of the discourse in order to address Di Cicco: the entire poem is an intense and persistent address to the younger man by Gasparini. Nevertheless the apostrophe only stresses the duplicity of the receiver: Di Cicco on the one hand and the Canadian reader on the other. The poem is therefore like a dramatic dialogue, in the sense that it is staged. Generally literature is supposed to be overheard, but eavesdroppping is not necessary when the characters are screaming. Di Cicco and Gasparini have been very loud in their anguished cries over the human condition.

It is a distinctive feature of Italo-Canadian poetry that made us select "Il sangue" by Gasparini, for many among the most effective poems are dedications reinforced by inchoative and hyperbolic apostrophes. To a reader they sound rhetorical but there is more here than figures of speech. Our *declinatio* takes us to a poem by Filippo Salvatore, an impressive Italian-Canadian intellectual and one of the more rhetorical of these ethnic writers. From the long apostrophe, "A Giovanni Caboto," the following lines seem to be significant:

> *Giovanni, ti hanno eretto*
> *un monumento, ma ti hanno cambiato nome:*
> *qui ti chiamano John.*[6]

It would seem that even the great Italian explorer does not escape the fate of the immigrant. The English might erect a monument in your honour, but they will change your name. The common ground of these two works, and many other apostrophic poems is the duplicity of language. If the characters on stage scream it is because they want to survive, because they do not want to die, to disappear. To abandon the language of your forefathers is to begin to die. For this reason the apostrophic poems must illustrate the clash of the old language of life and the new language of death. As a title, "Il sangue" is better than the English, blood. The two languages must clash; Italian-Canadian writers may work in English or French, but many titles, images and expressions remain Italian. Filippo Salvatore's translations for his own poems brings out this clash of languages.[7]

The title, "Il sangue," fulfills the added function of suggesting a greater intimacy and a need to tone down the meanings that would, if in English, emphasize the referent. It is obvious that "Il sangue" transforms the negative sign *blood* into a positive one. The reading of the poem confirms this observation and furthermore tends to show that, especially in the case of Italian-Canadian poetry, the experience of language is more important than the language experience:

> *The blood that moves through your language*
> *moves through mine.*
> *The heart that gives it utterance*
> *is ours alone.*
>
> *Come away from that cancer of neon*
> *with its running sores of money.*
> *The city's iron skyline*
> *bends before the structure of a poem.*
>
> *Our people work in the Tuscan fields,*
> *where the rain walks barefoot*
> *and the fragrance*
> *of the breathing earth*

rustles like the body of a woman
reaching out to you in sleep.
Let us string our mandolins and sing
O sole mio *every night!*

The joy is ours.
Strangled by a spaghetti stereotype,
an Italian is supposed to lay bricks.
You build poems with the stars.[8]

Given the apparent simplicity of the language in this poem, a first reading may lead to a single interpretation. On one level it clearly contains both the nostalgia for The Old Country (a feeling so often censored by puritanical and shortsighted critics) and an allusion to the latent racism of the Anglo-Saxon, dominating society (at least in Len Gasparini's poem if not in the real world). This single reading of "Il sangue" is, in our opinion, the wrong one because it succumbs to the referential illusion, the effect of mimesis, the naïve conception that leads some to believe that literature is a clear image or an imitation of life.

To begin with, the *blood* is more literary than real for it is the blood of language. Hence, from the start, the semiosis displaces the mimetic effect of the text. What makes this blood speak is, of course, a unique literary heart. Note also that this blood "moves," it does not flow. The substance of the human body here is both a metonymy of the person referring to his identity (in such clichés as "your own flesh and blood"), and a metaphor for racial distinction (identified by blood types). We also note here that the *heart* is unique, that is to say that there is only one heart that pumps the language for all Italian-Canadian poets.

Another digression seems useful here to study a surrealistic *amplificatio* of the Gasparini image which renews the concept of mystical body. The image is central in the sense that one heart shared by many bodies implies a greater death threat. Usually any elaboration of the Gasparini image converts the positive sign attached to the blood of language into a negative one. This is the case in the writing of a young feminist Italo-Canadian poet, Mary Melfi. The example that we have chosen is a section from a prose poem entitled "The Invalid":

> My heart and my womb have been properly attached to my body. My ex-husband's heart, my mother's heart and an entire dead baby whose mother I knew as a schoolgirl have also been properly attached to my body. They're resting on the table beside my hospital bed in their proper glass bottles.
>
> Liquids of all the colors of the rainbow (perhaps neon itself) are flowing into my bloodstream. My bed is surrounded by blue circles, gold circles, green and red circles of glass bottles. (I've been promised a blood transfusion as soon as the Red Cross workers call off their wildcat strike.)
>
> A glass bottle huge as a man is resting in the corner of the room. I'm sure this bottle contains my husband as it is black and it makes ugly noises in the night. I guess the genie wants to cast off his vows.
>
> A cord (with the colorings of a coral snake) attaches all the glass bottles to each other. Part of this cord is wrapped around my neck. In an attempt to pull the cord's head out of its electric socket I'd choke.[9]

So the image of the shared blood and shared heart is a bipolar one. At the positive end we have the literary case. When Gasparini writes *The heart that gives it utterance/is ours alone* we must conclude that the Italian blood is, at least in the area of language, and therefore inspiration, a privilege. At the negative end, a young woman implies perhaps that strong family ties are mainly a burden for the artist. In any case the blood of language and the heart of language appear as devices that generate textual material on the opposition life/death. What is most intriguing is that Gasparini — who seems to be so much on the side of life — relies heavily on the isotopy of death, that is to say on a cluster of images that lead us back to death connotations.

In the second stanza the poet derives his strength from a Baudelairian intertext.[10] Traditionally, the city with its artificial lights is obviously evil and the implication here prepares the opposition between rural Italy and urban North America where the night life seems to be generated by a non-European attachment to money.

The impact of the second stanza lies elsewhere. The images *cancer of neon* and *running sores of money* echo again a Dolorism not foreign to Dante nor to Baudelaire. The Italian artist seems permanently romantic and is convinced that he must be an exemplary sufferer. Those who suffer are the elite and it is often in this context that the positive polarity of blood images is achieved. Such is the case of Antonio D'Alfonso who in "Elegy of the Alcove" — a significant title — writes:

I am ancient. Of thick aristocratic blood.
And this blue blood inheritance overlooks
the universe of carnivorous experience.[11]

What is the nature of this "carnivorous experience"? Does it mean that the *sangue*, a characteristic of this literary aristocracy, is in itself a danger to the poet? As the voice of the poet, *il sangue* is symbol of suffering, as it was unforgettably treated by the philosopher, Sören Kierkegaard. This answer forces us to analyse this interpretation. Even if blood is used in its positive sense, it remains a curse. To verify this dimension of the poetic discourse we turn to Fulvio Caccia, an Italian-Canadian poet publishing in French:

Les ombres du passé
n'ont plus de prise sur moi

> *Ni leur sang, ni leur soumission*
> *n'étancheront ma soif*
> *Et Moloch est un bel animal*
> *plongeant sa dent de nacre*
> *dans la blessure.*[12]

Blood is part of the tradition that a poet rejects with difficulty. The presence of Moloch, usually a negative sign, is here converted to a positive one. The title of the poem "Nord" is a metonymy for Canada and indicates that for Caccia *sangue* has a more complex cluster of meanings than for Gasparini. Caccia from another generation, is using another linguistic sensibility and is aware of the hyberbole of his image. The meaning comes from the death of blood since the nord of the poet is determined by the word *métissé* which is given a positive sense:

> *Nord métissé, grand magnétiseur*
> *détourneur de langages*
> *tu fécondes le mythe*
> *dans ton sexe giboyant.*[13]

Suffering becomes the opposite of death, as is evident in many of the funeral poems produced by Italian-Canadians. It is clear that this opposition between suffering and death marks a break with a romantic tradition: for these poets death is not liberating. This concept of suffering seems to follow a classical tradition like that of Bossuet: "L'homme est un apprenti et la douleur est son maître." This view of suffering as a vital force cannot be explained simply by the Catholic background of the writers. Could this idea of suffering also be a result of the Latin world view meeting the North American one? The work of Italian writer, Cesare Pavese, sheds some light on this synthesis. It is significant that Pavese

*Your head is being kneaded
like dough in the noon
baker's hand. Your flesh
sizzles on the skewers
of your bones. Then evening
comes like a nervous sweat,
as anger condenses,
dew in cool grass.*

*You are alone on the highway to the sun.
Your north american education
has taught you how to kill a father,
but you are walking down an Italian
way, so you will surrender
and visit him in the hospital
where you will be accused
of wishing his death
in wanting a life
for yourself.*

*A scorpion's sting darkening
your heart buries July in Italy.* [15]

The patricide is symbolic, but it is a death linked to the immigrant experience. *Your north american education/ has taught you how to kill your father.* The child can have an independent life only by ritualistically killing the father, and this back in Italy. Does this mean rejecting Italy and things Italian? Is there not a danger here of committing cultural suicide in order to embrace North American values? These are the questions that Di Cicco, di Michele, Salvatore and other Italian-Canadian writers are exploring in their ongoing poetic discourse.

At the level of mimesis the problem can be expressed in the following terms: the ethnic poet struggles to assert himself, his particular experience and the value of his work. But when he is successful, when his work is accepted into the mainstream; has he not moved into another realm in which he is no longer himself? In "Il sangue" Len Gasparini uses images to express this dilemma: if you are *strangled by the spaghetti stereotype*, you are socially dead. If you overcome this problem to the point where there is no trace of Italian influence left in your work, you might *build poems with the stars* but your identity has been disolved into a context of cultural death. The treatment of death, a death in the family as in D'Agostino's "Wake", or mass death as in Joseph Pivato's "Friuli 1976: The Broken Wall," becomes a working hypothesis for the life and death struggle of a whole culture. There are many forms of death: perpetual marginalization, total assimilation, indifference or silence and invisibility.[16] In Italian-Canadian writing there are many examples that explore these questions. Antonino Mazza with "Death in Italy," Pier Giorgio Di Cicco with "Father," Filippo Salvatore with "La mia guerra," or other poems by Romano Perticarini could be read in this light.

In world literature there are examples of writers who have tried to transform the values of their native culture into their new literary language: Joyce, Kafka, Conrad and Nabokov. Can Italian-Canadian writers make this model work in this country in order to deal with the danger of death and oblivion? Pier Giorgio Di Cicco has achieved some success with a conscious process of trying to combine the Mediterrenean and the Nordic cultures. He explains that the very title of *The Tough Romance* captures the merger of the Italian and the North American:

> Il titolo stesso incapsula, per così dire, la mia sensibilità in tutte le mie poesie, implica una sensibilità mediterranea, temprata dall'ambiente nord americano. Credo che questa sia la conclusione logica dell'essere Italo-Canadese, nel senso migliore. Intendo *romantico* in termini mediterranei, in termini di luce... L'opposto dell'ethos celtico. Come sai *tough* vuol

dire un duro in italiano... Queste tensioni sono nel cuore di
Tough Romance...[17]

It is this tension that is helping Italian-Canadian poets
produce some of the most exciting collections of poems
of the 1980's.

NOTES

1 Saro D'Agostino, "Wake," in *Roman Candles*, ed. P.G. Di Cicco (Toronto: Hounslow Press, 1978), pp. 65-66.

2 Joseph Pivato, "The Arrival of Italian-Canadian Writing," *Canadian Ethnic Studies*, 14, no. 1 (1982), 131.

3 Pier Giorgio Di Cicco, "The Man Called Beppino," in *The Tough Romance* (Toronto: McClelland and Stewart, 1979), p. 11.

4 Pier Giorgio Di Cicco, "Donna italiana," *op. cit.*, p. 68.

5 Pier Giorgio Di Cicco, "Such Days," *Flying Deeper into the Century* (Toronto: McClelland and Stewart, 1982), p. 91.

6 Filippo Salvatore, *Suns of Darkness* (Montreal: Guernica, 1980), p. 16.

7 Filippo Salvatore, *op. cit.*, p. 17.

8 Len Gasparini, "Il sangue," in *Breaking and Entering: New and Selected Poems* (Oakville: Mosaic Press/Valley Editions, 1980), p. 68.

9 Mary Melfi, "The Invalid," in *A Queen Is Holding a Mummified Cat* (Montreal: Guernica, 1982), p. 21.

10 Charles Baudelaire, "Recueillement," in *Les Fleurs du Mal*, ed A. Adam (Paris: Garnier, 1961), p. 189.

11 Antonio D'Alfonso, "Elegy of the Alcove," *Black Tongue* (Montreal: Guernica, 1983), p. 23.

12 Fulvio Caccia, "Nord," in *Irpinia* (Montreal: Triptyque/Guernica, 1983), p. 19.

13 *Op. cit.*, p. 19.

14 Marco Fraticelli, *Instants* (Montral: Guernica, 1979), p. 52.

15 Mary di Michele, "How to Kill Your Father," in *Bread and Chocolate* (Ottawa: Oberon Press, 1980), pp. 35-36.

16 Marco Micone, *Gens du Silence* (Montreal: Québec/Amérique, 1982).

17 "Intervista a Pier Giorgio Di Cicco," in *Argomenti Canadesi*, ed. A. Lorenzini, Rome, Italy, 1978.

ROBERT BILLINGS

Contemporary Influences on the Poetry of Mary di Michele

I

During the last few years, Mary di Michele has emerged as one of Canada's finest and most widely-read young poets. Her reputation has grown steadily and, more importantly, been deserved. The rapid and impressive development of her poetics from the tentative lyrics in *Tree of August* (Three Press, 1978) to the meditations written in " a new language of passion and experience"[1] that appear in *Necessary Sugar* (Oberon, 1983) and *Moon Sharks* — working title — (McClelland and Stewart, 1986) suggests not only that she is a poet who has already made her mark in Canadian poetry, but also that she is one of the few poets of her generation who may be counted upon to be giving us fine work several years from now.[2]

It is always fascinating ten, twenty, thirty or more years after a poet has established such a reputation to look back and see exactly how, why, and under what circumstances it came about. In that exploration, contemporary accounts play a role in determining precisely what amalgam of factors and influences — some conscious, some accidental — produced a particular kind of writer and writing. Indeed, entire literary periods are sometimes examined (and sometimes created) from disparate information about chance meetings, authors' libraries, friendships, politics, reviews and reviewers. It may be most difficult to deal with such elements of literary history during the time the poet is writing the work that establishes her reputation: the influences are too new; the accidents keep happening. It is equally true, however, that sometimes it is possible to see clearly that a certain set of circumstances has arisen and will continue to exert an influence on what is written. More often than not, this begins with accidents and becomes a conscious attempt on the part of a few writers to modify contemporary assumption and practice.[3]

A group of poets with the potential to exert such an influence appeared in Toronto during the late 1970s and early 1980s. As with all such groups, its origins were quite accidental, and the result of circumstances that could not have been forseen. Now, almost ten years later, each of the members of that group has published at least one critically acclaimed book, and each still looks to the others and to the others' work for inspiration, guidance, friendship, criticism, new directions, and — not least — "a great deal of mutual affection and respect."[4] And the group has expanded: it now counts among its members more poets who happen to live in Toronto, as well as what might be called "charter members" in various parts of the country. Of course, they do not all write the same *kind* of poetry, but they have in common enough influences and aesthetic preoccupations to be a recognizable group. Di Michele is part of this group, and there is little doubt that to her participation in it she owes a large debt for the particular ways her poetics — content and style, manner and matter — have developed during the last ten years.

It is the purpose of this paper to examine the circumstances in which this group was formed, to determine why and how it has achieved the status of being influential and, in particular, to demonstrate the influence on di Michele of both the members of the group and of their work. Four poets, all of them women, emerge as the most important and continuing contemporary influences: Roo Borson, Susan Glickman, Bronwen Wallace, and Carolyn Smart. As we will see, some male poets also belong to the group — indeed, it was Pier Giorgio Di Cicco who was the catalyst in bringing many of the poets together — but it is these four women whose impact on di Michele both personally and through their work has been a vital, at times even a sustaining force. I will examine, in turn, the development of this group, and the work of each of them. It will be shown that di Michele's development as a poet was and remains in no small way influenced by this "support group of peers."[5]

II

In 1974 di Michele took a Masters degree in English and Creative Writing from the University of Windsor, where she had come under the tutelege of Joyce Carol Oates. Of her work at this time, di Michele has said:

> I think I was quite resistant to a lot of the things I could have learned from her... I had a sort of academic, objective approach to what I was trying to do, and I tended to deny personal experience and feeling and consciously tried to seek a universe of experience — that's not the way you get there; the only way you get there is by examining your own experience first... I talk about it now as a "resistance" because I wasn't susceptible, I couldn't learn, I didn't have the experience to understand what she was telling me.[6]

It is not, of course, unusual for young poets to have this kind of "academic, objective approach" to their work. Di Michele began to realize the importance of the experience that, from hindsight, she says she needed when, after more time in Windsor and brief periods in London, Ontario and Vancouver, she moved back to Toronto in 1976. During a visit home at Christmas, in 1975, she was introduced to Pier Giorgio Di Cicco by Tom Wayman, who had been Writer in Residence at Windsor. It is Di Cicco who is the catalyst here. The friendship between him and di Michele developed slowly, but his influence on her work eventually became an important one, especially in regard to finding ways to express the experience of the Italian immigrant in the North American city.[7] For our purposes here, an important factor is that Di Cicco opened up to her "a huge loose network of acquaintances... within which many friendships deepened."[8] In part, this network developed casually; poets and other friends met in cafés, at dinner parties, or at readings. For example, Borson recalls seeing di Michele for the first time:

> ... at a reading by Giorgio somewhere in the northern part of the city. It was probably in a library. I had heard her name mentioned — as a friend of Giorgio's who also wrote poetry. This was shortly after I moved to Toronto, possibly '77 or '78. At that point she looked very Italian: long red-gold hair, brillant lipstick and eye shadow, a droopy black shawl. We weren't introduced that night, but a few weeks or months later I though I recognized her at Harbourfront, approached and asked if she was Mary di "Miss Shelley" (everyone without Italian seems to mispronounce it that way at first) and she replied that she was but that her name was "Meek Eh Lay." And so we met.[9]

A major instrument of the network of friendship that developed was a workshop or "Sunday Salon," as some of the participants call it, that was held at Di Cicco and Carolyn Smart's apartment near the corner of Eglinton Avenue and Mount Pleasant Road. These two met in 1978 during a course Di Cicco was teaching at Three Schools, an ad hoc "fly-by-night offshoot" of the bookstore, Other Books, at Bloor Street West and Brunswick Avenue. This workshop, "jokingly dubbed the Highrise School of Poetry,"[10] was modelled on a group that had met at Joe Rosenblatt's house on Green-sides Avenue. Since the dispersal of that group, young poets met casually on streetcorners or at the Selby Hotel on Sherbourne Street (a famous watering-hole for Ernest Hemingway and several generations of Canadian writers), but they were starved for the kind of serious discussion about poetry that social occasions sometimes prohibit. The rather disparate group that met on Eglinton seemed to have in common only a dedication to poetry and an ambition to write the best work they could. Usually present were di Michele, Di Cicco, Smart, Borson, Kim Maltman (who was and continues living with Borson), Barry Dempster, and A.F. Moritz.[11]

It is not difficult to imagine the importance of the relationships that developed out of this series of accidents. One has only to think of the value to a young writer of a group of peers intensely interested in the same things and whose members live within a short subway or streetcar ride of each other. I doubt if any of them foresaw precisely the importance of what was happening. They were all, at that time, young poets who were quickly becoming veterans of the literary magazines, but who were not ready or able to take visible and influential places on Canadian poetry's stage. For example, di Michele had finished the poems in *Tree of August* (which she has described as "very early work"[12]) and, with much encouragement from Di Cicco, was beginning to form the sequence of poems about her family and the lot of the Italian immigrant daughter that would become *Bread and Chocolate*. Di Cicco had been publishing small books with very small presses, but was about to publish *The Tough Romance* (McClelland and Stewart, 1978); Borson had published *Landfall* (Fiddlehead, 1977) and was about to make a quantum leap in the writing of *A Sad Device*; Dempster was beginning to write the poems for *Fables for Isolated Men* (Guernica, 1982), a book that would gain him a nomination for the Governor General's Award. These young poets knew each other and liked each other's work at a time when each of them was, as it were, serving an apprenticeship, paying dues. The "Highrise School of Poetry" eventually petered out due to "obscure tensions,"[13] but it influenced di Michele in a number of important ways. Her work to this point had often been anecdotal, still "academic and objective." The work of Di Cicco, Borson, and Moritz exposed her to various influences, notably surrealism: Di Cicco had, since 1975, been reading and recommending the poetry and aesthetics of Latin American poets; Borson had brought with her from California the influence of American "deep image" poets such as James Wright, Robert Bly, and W.S. Merwin, as well as that of Robert Bringhurst, under whom she had studied at the University of British Columbia; Moritz was able to engage in long conversations on topics ranging from George Oppen to Northrop Frye.[14] Thus, the workshop left di Michele with ideas, influences, and friendships she retains. For example, she recalls that it was Maltman

> who loaned me his copy of Cesare Pavese's *Hard Labour* which influenced me immensely, especially in writing the *Bread and Chocolate* poems. Roo feeds me spiritually, as if I could read her and at the same time close my eyes and listen to a symphony made by natural instruments, the sea, the rain, the wind in branches and also something like the solar wind or the music of the spheres we only know as ideas. She makes them palpable.[15]

Smart sheds further light on this time when she says,

> I was insecure about my work, about my voice, and very undirected as to my possibilities as a writer... It was an enormous relief for me to meet Mary who seemed to share many of my concerns and was at a similar insecure point in her own

career... Mary and I were writing... about similar issues and voicing similar concerns. We were beginning to write as women, as I see it now.[16]

Although the workshop ended, the network of friends continued to exist and to expand. A regular meeting place was Harbourfront where, under the leadership of Greg Gatenby, the Tuesday evening reading series was beginning to gain its current international status as the major Canadian venue for public readings. After the readings, a group consisting of Gatenby, the evening's featured readers, the young literati, and other members of the audience would adjourn to a bar (usually the Hayloft on Front Street near Yonge to engage in various levels of camaraderie, literary gossip, and discussions of poetry. Di Michele and the other poets I have mentioned were "regulars" at these evenings. One remembers, for example, the Hayloft crowded with people who included W.S. Merwin, Leon Edel, Gatenby, di Michele, Borson, Maltman, Dempster, Di Cicco, David Donnell, and others, all of them drinking, laughing, telling stories.

The group also met regularly for other social occassions. Di Michele remembers that

> a group of us... would often have dinner together and read our current work to each other. We didn't workshop anything, but I think we've influenced each other by a kind of osmosis of ideas and textures and styles.[17]

It was during this time that the group also began to expand. Deliberate meetings at various houses or apartments, accidental meetings in cafés may have seen gathered together any or all of the poets, and may have included Robert Priest, Daniel David Moses, Libby Scheier, Peter Such, Dennis Lee, or Jan Conn or Erin Mouré when they were visiting from Vancouver, and other writers of varying age and accomplishment.[18]

It is now late 1979. We have seen a lot happen during the previous three years; not only the fortunate accidents that created a group of young poets, but also a number of specific influences on di Michele and her work. The next years will see this group continue to meet, and the addition of, to di Michele especially, two important new members: Bronwen Wallace and Susan Glickman.

Bronwen Wallace was at this time editor of the literary magazine, *Quarry*. She had been at Windsor during di Michele's time there, but the two had met only casually at a party; no strong attachment had developed. Wallace accepted several of di Michele's poems for *Quarry*, and the two began to correspond.[19] Soon, another fortunate accident occurred. Wallace had had a manuscript, *Marrying into the Family* accepted by Oberon Press, which was going to run it with a series of drawings. That project did not work out, but in the meantime Oberon had received di Michele's manuscript, *A Strange Grace* and decided that its first section, "Bread and Chocolate," could be paired with Wallace's manuscript: "The editors thought our family poems completed each other and would make a good book, also a safer risk for relatively unknown poets."[20] The book was published in September, 1980.

Living as she did (and does) in Kingston, Ontario, Wallace was, of course, not part of the group that had been expanding since 1976. Now, she became one of its first major "charter members," poets who did not live in downtown Toronto but who were friends with ones who did. Through di Michele, Wallace became one of these. After their double book was published, the two women travelled together to give promotional readings from it; Wallace stayed at di Michele's when she was in the city. As is the case with di Michele's friendships with Borson, Glickman, and Smart, the one with Wallace

continues to be a significant influence on both participants. Wallace can say,

> it's through my women friends that I survive. It's not that
> these relationships are "better than" those I share with my
> lover, my son or my male friends. It's just that they're ab-
> solutely necessary to my survival. Period... We're speaking
> with the authority of female human beings. As a poet I
> couldn't do this without Mary and the others. One more
> snide, time-warp, patently sexist review and I'd probably
> quit. But because I see us as a group, I am able to appreciate
> and work on my own strengths as a writer.[21]

And di Michele can respond:

> How can I ever thank Bronwen Wallace enough, for her intel-
> ligence, her enlightenment, her courage? I'm in awe of this
> woman who has such adult assurance and knowledge, with a
> child's sense of play, of fun.[22]
>
> I admire this woman immensely both as a poet and
> friend. Her work is characterized by its intelligence and its
> compassion and its social vision. Because she is at the center
> of this culture she can do many things in terms of describing
> and analyzing it, that someone, introverted and as an immi-
> grant somewhat on the fringe, finds more difficult.[23]

The phrases, "the authority of female human beings" and "at the center of this culture" imply important developments in di Michele's progress, especially
the kind of feminism toward which she had begun to
move at this point. It is true that she had always been "a
feminist writer" (as we shall see later, *Bread and Chocolate* and *Mimosa and Other Poems* display one kind of
feminism; *Necessary Sugar* and *Moon Sharks*, others).
As she indicated in an interview Mary di Michele sees a
direct connection between "the struggle of the immigrant girl" and the feminism of the mature woman:

> **JP:** Your early poems in *Bread and Chocolate* deal with the
> struggle of the immigrant girl, your later work in *Necessary*

Sugar addresses the condition of women. Do you feel that your experience as an immigrant girl has helped you to have a better perspective as a woman writer?

MdM: I feel that it has made me more radical in my responses. My family situation was a very patriarchal one. Both my father and mother tried to make me conform, to behave and direct my expectations to a limited and very female role. Because I was unhappy with the constrictions of that role I rebelled. In this way my immigrant experience made me more radical. [24]

With the later influence of Wallace di Michele's perceptions of the role and possibilities open to a woman writer increased dramatically. Wallace describes feminism, in terms of her relationship with Borson, Glickman, Smart, and, in particular, di Michele, as follow:

As far as the 5 of us go, we're all feminists, obviously... I think all of us see feminism as a movement which is not necessarily gender-specific. It has to do with attempting to change a culture in which, for many historical reasons, the standard of one gender has been "accepted" as the universal or the "human"... Definitely, the main source of strength, new ideas, personal and political growth, friendship, love, support, encouragement, anger, challenge, meaning and just about anything else in my life for the last 15 years at least has been the feminist movement... Specifically, what I see happening poetically among us is the *conscious* attempt to forge a "new language of passion and experience" (Mary's phrase), a feminist vision that gets beyond stridency, anger at men, despair, self-absorption, etc. What Mary does specifically, I think, is to use the poem as a process of exposure by which the repressed, the new, the unsayable is finally spoken. This is "confessional" poetry with an important political and aesthetic difference in that the poet writes, not from a sense of her "peculiarity" or her isolation, but from her sense of collectivity and connectedness with other women... She is aware — and what's more she assumes that we agree — that a feminist view is not peculiar to a few crazy women, but merely a part of how any reasonably perceptive human being would look at the world. [25]

Again, Smart is able to contribute important facts to all of this. They involve di Michele's marriage, the birth of her daughter, Emily, and subsequent divorce:

> Mary, Bronwen and I all share the difficulties and joys of raising a child and trying to write at the same time. Sometimes it feels like it's going to tear me apart. We've all felt that. It continues to draw the three of us closer and to mold our work in a particular way.[26]

As we shall see in Section III, this "way" involves a knowing of, at once, the self, the family, the past and the present.

Susan Glickman recalls meeting di Michele and Borson at a street fair during the summer of 1979. She and Smart had met in Greece in 1973, but had lost touch until the date of that fair. It had been a year and a half since Glickman had returned to Canada from four years of study (including a first-class M.A. from Oxford) and work in Europe. She sees the meeting that day as "a turning point" in her life:

> Suddenly a whole world opened up for me of articulate interesting people my own age who were dead serious about poetry; serious in the way I needed, the way that made it alright to need poetry the way I needed it, made it more than acceptable — made it essential... I wonder whether Mary and Carolyn and Roo actually have any idea how much their companionship gave to me? That maybe I would have given up writing for the second time if I hadn't "clicked" with them?[27]

Perhaps for this reason Glickman is quite eloquent and expansive on the subject of the group:

> Because we've watched each others' work develop, we've become mentors to each other, the best kind of critics: the ones who know a poet's whole oeuvre and can see where she's going and why and want her to get there... Some of this I think is feminism; a shared enterprise of writing about the

world from a new perspective, which makes everything possible... and frees us from the whole modernist/post-modernist notion that language is dead, or that everything's already been said, the stories used up, and that nothing but the most radical dislocation of language or literary convention can revivify it. For us, the stories are just starting to be told.[28]

Glickman and di Michele have been friends for several years. Recently, di Michele's perceptions of her friendship with Glickman include an implied assessment of the fact that during 1983 Borson moved to California (where Maltman took up post-doctoral studies in physics at Berkeley) and Smart married and move to Elginburg, Ontario (ironically, just north of Kingston, where Wallace lives):

With the heart of the Toronto group having fragmented, people breaking up, moving away, being a single parent, I find myself now quite isolated. Susan is one of my closest friends. We talk, exchange books, ideas, regularly. She is a thoughtful writer and a clear thinker.[29]

What we have seen, then, is the development of a large network of friendships that combined the kinds of things any group of friends would do with a dedication to poetry that made this network a support group for several young poets. A key ingredient in this development was the fact that most of these young poets — including the five on whom I have focussed — were maturing very quickly. The achievement of maturity in a poet can never be isolated, be pinned down to a specific event or poem or influence. It is a quality that is acquired slowly, through hard work, and involves the maturity of the person as well as the finding of a voice, a style, a content that is compatible with that person's perceptions of the world. Di Michele began to achieve her maturity under the disparate influences I have traced, and out of all of those voices around her she has come to be closest to Borson, Wallace, Glickman, and Smart. They share a feminist outlook, an ambition to write as well as they are able, and a dedication to aesthetic principles and to poetry as a means of presenting them. Within the larger group, they form a smaller, and the resulting concentration of social, political, and poetic influences produces a definable approach to poetry, and books that, when read together, demonstrate the development of that approach.

III

After reading Section II, it may be a temptation to see di Michele, Borson, Glickman, Smart, and Wallace as one poet. This, however, is definitely not possible. A reading of their works reveals several similarities of outlook and various definable influences, but also five very distinct voices. It seems that "the new language of passion and experience" contains many inflections, tones, and syntactical and grammatical variations. It is a term we may accept because it is broad enough to be applied to all of these poets; it is a valid assessment of what they are trying to do, but it is not a language they *created* by consensus. It is, rather, an amalgam of the ones each poet, partly under the influence of the others, has come to employ. To see it as one language is to assign it several distinct properties, and to realize that it is capable of developing others. In the process of examining it, it is possible to not only discover those properties, but also to assess its validity as a language for poetry and for what Glickman calls "the stories that are just starting to be told." For the most part I will mention early examples of both of these elements and concentrate on their more mature forms.

It is Wallace who first put a mature version of this

language on paper. At least as early as the Fall of 1976 she was writing the poems that would become *Marrying into the Family*, a book that focuses on the lives of several female ancestors. The poems are straightforward narratives in which Wallace employs the facts of family history as a means of coming to know better both her heritage and herself. There emerges a strong connection between tradition and contemporary events, some of them approved of, some of them not. As an example, take "Stripping Furniture," a poem that operates on the notion that *Grandma painted the rocker/for each new baby* and that Wallace is now stripping away layers of paint, of the past, while preparing the chair for her own child:

> *I reach for the scraper*
> *slide back another layer*
> *pushing toward*
> *some afternoon in late summer*
> *supper warming on the stove*
> *kids playing on the porch   a baby*
> *crying in the back bedroom*
> *and a woman I begin to imagine*
> *with hair the colour of soft bare wood*
> *squatting heavily beside this rocking chair*
> *dipping her brush.*

This, like many of the poems in the book, is deceptively simple. The metaphor, of course, is memorable and highly appropriate; but the language Wallace uses to convey it is equally important. As we read through the works of the five poets here we will discover that each of them develops a forthright, straigthforward way of saying things, and of telling the stories of their lives and the world around them. This is the "passion" of the new language — not, of course, to be confused with eroticism, but rather to be accepted as a method, a voice, that relies for its authority on the honesty of the poet to both herself and the reader. It is in this sense an approach to language that is deliberately adopted and employed for the purpose of a particular kind of communication. *Marrying into the Family*, for example, alternates between employing the third and first person, a device that not only often links past with present grammatically, but also allows the narrative to develop in a way that validates the poet's perceptions of the particular kind of experience she is writing about. The story involves female ancestors and the poet's attempt to know and accept them; the language is direct utterance that allows such a search to be conducted personally and comment on that search to be introduced as an integral part of it.

Around this time di Michele was still in her "academic, objective" phase. It produced *Tree of August*, an uneven book that contains examples of the young poet's experiments with voice and form. The poems that work best are the ones that take either di Michele or her Italian family as their subjects. She could not have known at this point that to concentrate on these Italian subjects would allow her to eventually find her mature voice. Of the poems in the book, "Born in August" is the most important for our purposes:

> *Born in the fifth house*
> *under the sign of Leo*
> *on the sixth of August*
> *four years after Hiroshima,*
> *180 years after the birth*
> *of Napoleon Bonaparte,*
> *born Maria Luisa di Michele,*
> *baptized at Santa Lucia*
> *in an ancient town, Lanciano, the Abruzzi,*

> *scarred by cruel claws*
> *of war, the fangs of tyranny:*
> *Austerlitz, Auschwitz, Hiroshima,*
> *born with the rising sun*
> *the predator moon, a lion,*
> *born from my mother's dream*
> *when a rat nursed her face*
> *in the concentration camps,*
> *sucking the breast of famine*
> *my mother lost her teeth*
> *while I grew miniature bones*
> *like pearls in an oyster mouth.*

This is an early example of what the language of passion and experience will be. The insistence on emotion and its validity as both worthwhile and necessary combines with straightforward presentation, personal history, and a muscular rhythm. It is a confessionalist poet's first major step toward a mature voice.

Under the influence of the Highrise School and their other friendships, di Michele and Borson were at this time (1977-80) making rapid progress. Glickman and Smart were writing the books that would introduce them to us. All four were reading each other's work in draft. This is the point at which the group slowly becomes a group. The development of each member's poetics coalesces around a desire — perhaps a need — to perceive personal experience of the world as a worthy and appropriate subject. The language they will soon share begins to mature.

During these years Borson was writing *In the Smoky Light of the Fields* (Three Trees, 1980) *A Sad Device* (Quadrant, 1981) and *Rain* (Penumbra, 1980).[30] The first is a slim book of lyrics that present landscapes imbued with a moody atmosphere that creates an impression of awe and dread, of the numinous quality of

Nature and of being alive in the flesh in its presence. The language is richly metaphoric, but terse, sometimes imagistic, and usually concerns particular moments abstracted from time. It is not until *A Sad Device* that Borson is able to expand such moments and her method of linking them together into a more mature and expansive form. Not only are the poems generally longer, but they also present that numinous landscape through more fully developed and layered forms. The method often involves a combination of the first or second person singular with objectively presented perceptions of landscape. This device often separates the poet grammatically from the reader, but at the same time implies the belief in a shared universe of experience. Major examples include "Collected Landscapes," "At Night You Can Almost See the Corona of Bodies," "Moon," and "This is the Last Night." Overall, the book is a richly textured presentation of a world full of wonder and dread. As for its language, it is the kind of direct utterance that wants urgently to show a reader the characteristics of a particular view of Nature, and involves what Borson has called "emotional nuances one after another, stringing them together," and the fact that, for her, "the external and the internal worlds aren't separate."[31]

When we come to *Rain* we suddenly find Borson peopling her landscapes to a greater extent and relying on a more personal voice. *Rain* is one poem in twenty parts and combines first person observations with a narrative about friends on the West Coast. We find again what is quickly becoming Borson's world, a beautiful and forboding place in which the mind is subject to and sometimes equated with qualities of Nature. The "emotional nuances" are still strung together, but there is more worth and time assigned to personal history. The utterance is more direct, and concerned with telling a story. There is a new looseness, an acceptance of wider possibilities of speech that was absent from *A Sad Device*:

> *The way water does not bear up,*
> *the way rain crosses a landscape*
> *like locusts, their many bodies falling dead, the way*
> *I want to tell this story,*
> *the way water flows away,*
> *the way I want this story not to be able to bear up…*

While Borson was writing these three books, di Michele was working on *Bread and Chocolate* and *Mimosa and Other Poems*. Most of the poems in these books concern a kind of self-absolution in which she "exorcised a lot of the family ghosts and family devils."[32] It is through this process that she progresses in finding both her mature voice and the subjects — herself, the female artist — that still mark her work. *Bread and Chocolate* and "Mimosa" are two sequences that announce di Michele's independence from the traditions and pressures of her family. Through these poems she comes to terms with her childhood and adolescence, the experience of a first generation Italian immigrant daughter. This involves a tenet of feminism, indeed of any human rights movement: an insistence on the rights of the individual within the traditions, prejudices, and preconceptions of a particular group. The "story" is of di Michele herself, but to tell it she creates a persona that, as is the case with Wallace's *Marrying into the Family*, combines use of the first and third persons so that the past can be examined in the context of the present. The difference is that, whereas Wallace wants to know about and accept the past, di Michele wants to reject it or, at least, define herself in contrast to it. The two sequences are, therefore, narratives of experience.

In "Mimosa" she establishes a dialectic between two sisters that constitutes her first major exploration of dramatic narrative and allows her to experiment with personae. The increasing influence at this point of the other four poets, especially Wallace's feminism and Borson's surrealism and recently found possibilities of the first person, are accidents of time and place di Michele quickly absorbed and began to employ.

These influences can be seen in "Mimosa," and also in "Full Circle" and "A Fiction of Edvard Munch," poems that blend language, sentiment, and structure with a new maturity. By concentrating on the lives of two artists, Frida Kahlo and Munch, di Michele demonstrates what will be an ongoing interest in the process of art. By concentrating on that subject in the voices of two personae, she prefigures the approach she will increasingly apply to her own life, her own artistic process. The female poet living in the city, who is a single parent and, on a daily basis concerned with the various emotions and circumstances of such a situation will soon become the prime fiction, the informing voice, of di Michele's work. Exploration of the passion and experience of her adolescence, and of the lives of two troubled artists prepare her for her movement into a purer realm of confessionalism.

The relationship among all five of the poets was becoming increasingly closer when *Mimosa and Other Poems* was published in 1981. It is, therefore, not surprising to discover more similarities in their work. The "osmosis" about which di Michele has spoken was happening more quickly and more often. The cases of Smart and Glickman typify this.

Smart's two books of this time, *Swimmers in Oblivion* (York, 1981) and *Power Sources* (Fiddlehead, 1982) demonstrate her growing confidence and, when placed in the time-frame within which the Borson and di

Michele books just discussed were written, can be seen as evidence of "osmosis." The former book is, predictably, diffuse, the voice of the poet taking many different turns — in short, a first book containing poems written in several styles over several years, including tenure in the Highrise School of the late 1970s. Already, however, there exists the beginnings of the voice and the language she will come to see as her own, and an acceptance of personal history as a worthwhile subject. There are also here a number of narrative poems that tell the "stories" of the woman in the city, of relationship to men and to other women, and of the woman as artist. She, too, is working with personae, using them as voices to encompass personal experience and perceptions of an often dark, painful world. *Power Sources* is a much more confidently written book in the sense that, although much of it involves a search, a self-examination marked by doubt, the writing itself and the value assigned to personal experience are rarely questioned. Images of darkness, cold, night, and a dialectic of memory and forgetting mark her perceptions of her place in various kinds of relationships. There is more reliance on images and metaphor, although narrative retains an important place. The "stories" are ones the group of five now begin to write more frequently: the woman and the artist in the city attempting to cope with the various pressures of love, friendship, and daily life. A sense of alienation pervades many of these poems, but it is a quality Smart treats directly and honestly:

> *Dark spaces behind some trees,*
> *filled with the voice of a thousand frogs*
> *all crying to the same rhythm,*
> *or do we force some rhythm out of it,*
> *some sense, the way we force ourselves*
> *to see a pattern in life*

in order to be able to go on living it,
day follows night follows day.

This directness continues to develop in Smart's recent work, as for example in "Flying," a poem that tells Smart's perceptions of a birthday party for di Michele (and is dedicated to her):

Bone and the spark of cells
is all we have ever had
We see so clearly what we want
from a simple life
Language and touch bring us closer
to what we once knew before fear
The belief in tenderness   innocence

Glickman's *Complicity* (Véhicule, 1983) demonstrates close ties with the work of the other Toronto poets, especially di Michele and Borson. Generally, she, too, writes about the woman in the city, and her search for a kind of life that includes enough affection and self confidence to overcome the often confining elements of day to day life, as in "Underground":

But where are they going, those other travellers?
Sitting across from them on the subway
we deduce a life from dentures,
from worn shoes and wedding rings.
Right thumb and forefinger screw the ring 'round
*   and 'round*
like the lid on a child-proof bottle.

It is not easy for the poet, given her acute perceptions of the world about her, to cope with a city full of potential friendships of varying degrees. One poem, "Living Alone," operates on the notion that noisy appliances are sometimes one's only companions: *You wake up dreaming you're asleep in the fridge, /there's so much white space beside you.* Generally, *Complicity* is filled with images of constriction: a mousetrap under a radiator, darkness, buttons, rings, shrinkage, crawling, traps, winter, and this:

> *All I want is everything —*
> *not this ceaseless tide wearing its heart on its sleeve*
> *but the whole surround: high rocks*
> *from which to see the sunrise, a boat,*
> *blue-sweatered fishermen obliviously at work,*
> *a clump of queen-anne's lace, wild iris,*
> *and those small pinks that fight between boulders*
> *for air, just a little air.*

Glickman's recent work continues these themes, and the language she employs has become a mature version of the new language. It is a decidedly urban vision, filled with cafes, street scenes, and vivid but tenuous moments of comfortable relationship with people and surroundings:

> *I am tired of touring through love, that hot city;*
> *its vendors and touts, its bazaars full of*
> *   second-hand goods.*
> *Don't tell me the carpet can fly, I just want to see*
> *its exquisite flaw, its knotted*
> *human heart.*

Her search, like those of the other four poets, continues. Quite recently she has begun writing poems that happen outside downtown Toronto, poems that rely on her travels during the 1970s. This, of course, is part of a search for oneself and one's place in the world through memory — a method we have seen all of the poets here have in common.

We come now to the final phase of our examination. Di Michele's *Necessary Sugar* and *Moon Sharks*, Borson's *The Whole Night, Coming Home* (McClelland and Stewart, 1984), and Wallace's *Signs of the Former Tenant* (Oberon, 1983) comprise prime examples of what the group is trying to accomplish in terms of both content and language. Each story is personal, based on the poet's commitment to the validity of personal experience, and involves a search for both self and self's place within particular circumstances. The voices are different, but the approaches are similar.

Wallace's book was the first of these to be completed. It is a long, wide-ranging book in which she deals with many kinds and stages of relationship and communication. The poet's childhood, adolescence, lovers, family, children are all important subjects. As was the case with *Marrying into the Family*, this book often uses memory as a device to explore, to narrate. The general impression is of flux, a world in which attachments, perceptions, and emotions should be realized and defined at particular moments or else lost. These are *the shifts no instrument can measure*: *lost dreams, uneasy spring*, "The Country of Old Men," "The Heroes You Had as a Girl," and "Signs of the Former Tenant." Despite Wallace's hope that her *life/is slowly tidying itself*, she remains acutely aware of the "muddles" and clutter of daily life and her need to perceive the mystery, beauty, and hope within that context. Many of the poems deal specifically with women, women tempted into affairs, coping with unruly children, sitting in silent rooms. Most striking is "A Simple Poem for Virginia Woolf" and most poignant the sequence, "The Cancer Poems" about the slow death of a close friend. Ultimately, although *all change is a kind of death*, change is preferable to constriction, stagnation, acceptance. In a sense, Wallace's language reinforces this notion. It is a narrative language that allows the stories to be told straightforwardly and to be injected with the poet's perceptions so that story and perception blend into new wholes, unique entities drawn from the particular circumstances of one woman's life.

In 1980, Borson was buildings on the method she discovered by writing *Rain*. Influenced by Kim Maltman's *Branch Lines* (Thistledown, 1982), she began experiments through which, as she says, she "stumbled across a way of writing about the landscape and mood of the place where I grew up, and also, coincidentally, I had found a way of writing about growing up."[33] Her *The Whole Night, Coming Home* consists of two cycles of poems — the first in verse, the second in prose — that examine her childhood and adolescence in Southern California. We enter again the world we now recognize as her own; the difference lies in its presentation. Up to and including *A Sad Device* the landscapes had been more or less impersonal; now they are linked strongly to both a specific, named place and to the poet herself. In this sense, she has adopted a form of confessionalism, a reliance on personal history as an informing metaphor that can be employed to present and to comment on a given time and place. Memory, of course, plays a vital role in this process; and it is evident that by focusing on it Borson has both developed the voice she used in *Rain* and come to perceive personal experience as a thing that may be treated directly, without abstracting it. This method is evident in both sections of the book, but particularly in the second, "Folklore," a long series of prose poems that focuses on her family. Of this sequence, she has said that, in 1982, the lines she "was writing wanted to be fluid and prosy and lyrically conversational. They didn't want to be broken; the pause structure of poetry was too formal, intense, slow."[34] This is an adequate definition of her current style, her current version of the new language. The interest in narrative, conversation, and fluidity does not discount the surrealistic effect of "stringing together" "emotional nuances," indeed the two methods complement each other.

At the time Borson was beginning to examine all of these possibilities, di Michele was finishing her experiments with personae in *Mimosa and Other Poems*. The result of her subsequent focus on her own life was *Necessary Sugar* and, later, *Moon Sharks*. The language is noticably looser than in *Mimosa and Other Poems*, and the focus on di Michele's personal experience unswerving. The two books mark her movement simultaneously into realms of genuine confessionalism and straightforwardly presented feminism — thus what Wallace has noticed is "confessional poetry with an important political and aesthetic difference." Poems such as "Day Journey into Night," "The Body Electric," "How I Make My Body Disappear," "The Dragons of Sullivan Street," and "Romance of the Cigarette" display a need to come to terms with what it means to be a woman and an artist in the contemporary city. The general impression created is of a kind of actuality that must be confronted daily, honestly, and with a well-wrought blend of toughness and idealism. The repeated focus on the elements of relationship with men, especially on sex, are understandable in the context of a dissolving marriage, but the point may be that di Michele has accepted direct treatment of the subject as the keystone of her view of the woman in the city. In doing so it seems she has become at once confessionalist poet and a poet who is able to strike responsive chords in her readers because she focuses intelligently on those elements of human interaction. There is joy, yes, but more often she presents us with the blacker, moodier side of relationship, as in "Bloody Marys," or "The

147

Wheat and the Chaff,'' in which she meditates on her infant daughter in a passage that demonstrates both preoccupation with relationships and the way di Michele has come to use the new language: the conversational tone, the insertion of striking images at what seem to be precisely the correct places:

She will be the woman who can abandon
her body without fear
of hitting bottom or
the wooden floor with its glistening
sweat of wax
slapping her face.

Reminds me of a time before
I began sleeping under the bed
pushed out by the man who prefers
to keep his hands on glossy photographs
in magazines
or blond secretaries in high heels,
you know the type, hot little numbers,
smoking cigarettes
on the long slim stems imported from France,
glasses of white wine.

Generally, then, *Necesary Sugar* is a book di Michele needed to write because of what was happening in her life. For our purposes, the writing of it allowed her to build on the methods she had been experimenting with in earlier books, and thereby discover both the subject and the language that, it now seems, will comprise her mature voice. Also, at this time the group of five were becoming increasingly close and sharing a growing awareness of what both a woman and poetry may be and accomplish. For di Michele this was crucial. Her continuation, in *Moon Sharks*, of many of the elements found in *Necessary Sugar* demonstrates that she has found herself, or a persona of herself through which much can be said. Some of the poems are decidedly more lyrical and, partly under Borson's influence, employ the context of landscape. The focus, however, is squarely on di Michele and, by implication, accomplished partly through combining the first and second persons, everyone who searches for a perception of the world that allows enough room for sensation, intelligence, wonder, fear, humour, and joy. A synthesis of these elements is rare; usually the story involves a search for an appropriate attitude or response. One time a synthesis does occur is in "Sex and Death," a poem about salmon approaching spawning grounds (note that the subject is sex, the language at once conversational and richly metaphoric):

> *This is how love became blind,*
> *dashing its brains out*
> *against rocks,*
> *reciting in an unwholesome, hooked mouth,*
> *sweet* nada, *endearments, proposals.*
> *These are the dead whose appetites are alive,*
> *decadents fond of the beach*
> *and the beauty of blonde boys...*
>
> *The salmon seem to decompose as they swim*
> *in horrible vacancies of flesh,*
> *a sexually transmitted leprosy,*
> *but the eggs are gilt,*
> *radiant with phosphorescent milk.*

IV

I have traced the development of di Michele's increasing awareness both of what was happening in contemporary Canadian poetry and of the possibilities of her own work between 1974 and 1984. What emerge from the several possible influences she encountered during this time are close personal, poetic, and political ties with four other young poets. Together, the five participated in a kind of "osmosis" by which each one influenced the others. They have come to write about themselves and, by implication, the persona or fiction of the woman and the poet in contemporary society. What they have come to recognize as a common language is in fact an amalgam of several tones, inflections, and constructions, but all of them employed for the purpose of telling the "stories that are just staring to be told," the stories of contemporary women. Each of the five has developed a distinct, even a recognizable voice; but they remain a group because those voices treat similar elements of experience with a directness and honesty that have so far been absent from Canadian poetry. Through their work a "new language of passion and experience" has come into being and begun to be perceived as at once valid and necessary. If the best critic is time, their work over the course of the next several years may prove to be as important to Canadian poetry as it will be to themselves. And that, of course, is their goal.

NOTES

1 Letter from Wallace, 26 Sept. 1984.

2 For a general examination of di Michele's work up to and including *Mimosa and Other Poems*, see my "Discovering the Sizes of the Heart: The Poems of Mary di Michele" in *Essays on Canadian Writing* 27 (Winter 1983-84), pp. 95-115.

3 One is able to think immediately of several examples of this. Canadian ones include: the friendship among Scott, Edgar, Carman, Roberts, etc; the McGill movement; the group around Contact Press (Layton, Souster, Dudek); the Tish revolution in Vancouver; the group of poets that gathered around The Coach House Press.

4 Letter from Borson, 26 Sept. 1984.

5 Letter from Glickman, 24 Sept. 1984.

6 An interview I did with di Michele, taped on 16 Aug. 1981. Almost three years later, in another interview, di Michele feels the same:

JP: At the University of Windsor you studied with novelist Joyce Carol Oates. Did this have a strong effect on your writing?

MdM: Yes, a very profound effect, as a matter of fact, although not immediately because the negative aspect of my academic training was that it made me concentrate primarily on intellectual information and not pay sufficient attention to my own experience. She essentially taught me that a writer has to dive into her own experience. I already knew about intellectual subjects, but I needed to be put in touch with myself. That was important. I think that only writers can guide other writers with this. It seems that academics neglect this approach, especially with their bias for the New Criticism.

(Interview with di Michele by Joseph Pivato, *Vice Versa*, Vol. I, No. 5-6 (June 1984), p. 22.)

7 *Ibid*. In her letter to me of 30 Sept. 1984, di Michele adds: "As a feminist I don't think that Giorgio is in opposition to me but rather a very necessary part of the dialectic of social thinking and discovery. I think we complement each other. There have been some raised feminist eyebrows at my working with him on an anthology which is essentially a dialogue in poetry which reflects the changes that feminist ideas have caused in men-women relationships. The love lyric has got to catch up." In late 1984 this anthology had received a favourable response from McClelland and Stewart, but no decision to publish had been taken.

8 Letter from Borson, 26 Sept. 1984.

9 *Ibid*.

10 *Ibid*.

11 Some of the information in this paragraph comes from conversations with Moritz (on 6 Oct. 1984) and Di Cicco (on 7 Oct. 1984).

12 Interview, 16 August 1981.

13 Letter from Borson, 26 Sept. 1984.

14 In 1977 di Michele read at Harbourfront with Len Gasparini, Antonino Mazza, Saro D'Agostino and Pier Giorgio Di Cicco who was then collecting poems for *Roman Candles: An Anthology of Poems by Seventeen Italo-Canadian Poets*

(1978). It seems that it was Antonino Mazza, who had studied under Umberto Eco at Pisa, who introduced the group to the poetry of Cesare Pavese by reading Pavese's "South Seas" one night. The influence of Pavese on this group of poets deserves a separate study in itself.

15 Letter from di Michele. In her letter of 26 Sept. 1984 Borson relates an anecdote that a Canadian magazine in which both she and di Michele had poems switched their contributor's notes "so that she could claim to have been born in California and I in the Abruzzi. We were delighted and proud that the random universe had chosen to play this little joke and had picked us out as being not only related but interchangeable. That about sums up our feelings for each other."

16 Letter from Smart, 9 Oct. 1984.

17 Letter from di Michele, 30 Sept., 1984.

18 Each of the young poets here have published a book and is developing a wider audience: Priest, *The Visible Man* (Unfinished Monument, 1980), *Sadness of Spacemen* (Dreadnaught, 1982), *The Man Who Broke Out of the Letter X* (Coach House, 1984); Moses, *Delicate Bodies* (blewointment, 1981), Scheier, *The Larger Life* (Black Moss, 1983); Conn, *Red Shoes in the Rain* (Fiddlehead, 1983). Mouré's work is well known, and gained a nomination for the Governor General's Award in 1979.

19 The poems appear in *Quarry* 27:4 (1978), and includes ones from both *Tree of August* and *Bread and Chocolate*.

20 Letter from di Michele, 30 Sept. 1984.

21 Letter from Wallace.

22 Di Michele, ed. *Anything Is Possible: A Selection of Eleven Women Poets* (Mosaic Press, 1984), p. 9. The anthology includes work from Borson, Marilyn Bowering, Conn, Lorna Crozier, di Michele, Glickman, Mouré, Scheier, Smart, Rosemary Sullivan, and Wallace.

23 Letter from di Michele.

24 Interview with di Michele by Pivato.

25 Letter from Wallace.

26 Letter from Smart. For an examination of the emotional and intellectual elements of parenthood and poetry, see Libby Scheier, "Creativity and Motherhood: Having the Baby *and* the Book" in *This Magazine* 18:4 (Nov. 1984), pp. 9-12.

27 Letter from Glickman.

28 *Ibid.*

29 Letter from di Michele.

30 *A Sad Device* was published after *Rain*, but written before it. See my "A Conversation with Roo Borson" in *Waves* 12:2-3 (Winter 1984) pp. 5-16.

31 *Ibid.*

32 Interview, 16 August 1981.

33 Letter from Borson, 30 Aug. 1984.

34 *Ibid.*

FULVIO CACCIA

The Italian Writer and Language

Translated by Martine Leprince

Lorsque la réalité nationale gît en lambeaux dispersés de toutes parts, l'individu émerge seul et commence à respirer. Les problèmes qui se posent alors à lui sont des problèmes de forme, c'est-à-dire des problèmes d'artifice.

Bertrand et Morin

The literature of immigrants now being written by Italians is making a strong showing in Canada. It spans both English and French and so realigns the balance of power between them. "There are no innocent languages," states Régis Debray in *Le Scribe*.[1]

Under what conditions is this literature of immigration being written, and to what extent do these conditions reflect the political and linguistic conflicts between Quebec and the rest of Canada? These are questions I would like to explore in these pages. For it is indeed an exploration. Both the newness of this body of literature and its relative unity encourage such questions. Any talk about writing leads us back to a discussion on the relationship between literature and language. For this reason I prefer to use the expression *minority literature* in place of *immigrant literature*, which makes reference to the thematic level only. The term *minority literature* is better suited to express the problem of form I would like to elaborate on. I have borrowed this term from Kafka, as did Deleuze and Guattari in their penetrating study published in 1977 on the writer from Prague.[2] It is, in fact, within this perspective that I would like to add my observations.

According to the linguist Henri Gobard, a tetralinguistic model modifies our relationship with language. First, *vernacular language*, of rural and maternal origin. It signifies the *here and now*. Then there is *vehicular language*, urban, state-controlled, bureaucratic and commercial. This language is found everywhere and acts as a primary agent of deterritorialization. *Referential language* is the language of culture, the language of *over there*. Lastly, there is *mythic language*, the language of religion, of the *beyond*.[3]

The distribution of these languages varies from one group to another, depending on time and place. It operates in the manner of radio waves, with the same silences, jamming and interference. The playwright Marco Micone is one of those who has best expressed this linguistic dilemma. One of his characters, Mario, says in *Gens du silence*: "I speak Calabrian with my parents, French with my sister and my girlfriend, and English with my buddies."[4] Through his political theatre, Micone has tried to break down the wall of silence which for twenty years has stood between the French-speaking populace and the Italian immigrants.

Let us take a brief look at what each of these languages corresponds to for the second generation Italian writer. If we use the model cited above, the immigrant regional dialects are the vernacular language: Molisano, Sicilian, Calabrian, Neapolitan, etc. English would be the vehicular language for the majority, with the exception of 15% who were educated in French schools in Quebec. The vehicular language also corresponds to the first break with the vernacular maternal language, the first manifestation of change. This is what Deleuze and Guattari call the *primary deterritorialization*. English would also be the referential language for the majority of Italian Canadians. The referential language starts up the process of reterritorialization. I will come back to this point. Lastly, Italian corresponds to the mythic language.

The cards are dealt. How is the game organized in relation to the geography of creativity? Let us reexamine the data in light of the migratory experience. Italians, a minority group within a minority, straddling three cultures and three languages, maintain a complex relationship with language. This triangulation is rich in possibilities. In this respect, Italian culture is following the example of Quebecois culture which asserts itself as distinct from the English-Canadian model, which in turn is striving to break free from American influence.

Immigration was a traumatic experience for the majority of Italian families. The shock and pain of adaptation have reverberated in the tonality, the syntax and the rhythm of the dialect spoken by the parents, an ideal surface pounded by ancestral fears and famine, swept by invasions and drought. This dialect, an agglomeration of regional archaisms and Italian and English expressions, thus becomes, for the second generation, the language of remembrance and exile. For this reason it plays a role similar to that played by Yiddish for the Jews of the Diaspora, though without the same lengthy process of sedimentation. One can imagine what would have become of Calabrian or Sicilian, for example, if these dialects had been grafted onto English over seven centuries spent in urban ghettos.

Let us come back to the descendants of these immigrants. How do they react to this language fraught with the suffering of the past? They deny it, they repress it. The apprenticeship of the vehicular language and the frenetic adhesion to the values of a consumer-oriented society become the accepted means through which to make the break. But this break, this disconnection cannot last indefinitely. It demands a reconnection, a link on another level. The Toronto poet Mary di Michele states in a recent interview:

> When I look at my own experience... I see that at some point I wanted to identify myself with the intellectual and public world of English. I took English to be my own and wanted it because it seemed to me to be an escape from the kind of emotional morass of the Italian family. While at home my position was that of a daughter, I wanted more than the emotional life of a daughter, and later of a mother. I wanted an intellectual life too, so I embraced English as my salvation. On the other hand I am aware that Italian represents a side of my life charged with feeling, an emotional dimension, for this reason Italian words often come out in my work as if they came from another realm of experience or intensity of feeling.[5]

English, with the language of Shakespeare as a cultural horizon, is thus used by the Italian intellectual as a means of getting in touch with his past, of understanding it. It is through English that he will try to retrace the genesis of his rejection of the maternal language, from the first years of schooling (between 1955 to 1966), up to today. In fact, it is in this language that the majority of works will be written, as proven by the two English anthologies assembled by Di Cicco and Di Giovanni. It would be of interest to compare these two works with the anthologies prepared by Tonino Caticchio (a bilingual French-Italian edition), and the French anthology of D'Alfonso and myself.[6] The reader will note that a certain number of writers appear in all four books. Together these works operate as interchangeable prisms; each one highlights a particular aspect of the same reality seen from three different perspectives: Italian, Quebecois and English-Canadian. These simultaneous points of view, so dear to McLuhan, show the permeability of linguistic barriers.

However, even if English did exercise this double

function as both vehicular and referential language in the majority of Canadian provinces, it was not so for many Italians in Quebec. These people in fact went from English as vehicular language to French as cultural and referential language. Molière replaced Shakespeare as norm and model.

This change coincided with the strengthening of the political personality of Quebec and made itself felt most acutely at the time when the generation which is today in its thirties entered university. It should be noted that the Quebecois learned in the streets by this generation, was itself in a similar inferior relationship to official French, as was dialect to Italian; here we have a clear picture of the linguistic complexities which confronted the Italians in Montreal.

For the majority of Italian-Canadians, the relationship to normative Italian is included within this complex pattern. At once desired and detested, Italian, the mythic language, is also the language of power. The ability to speak Italian well is a mark of class, of social mobility. "The real Italian, the Italian of the upper classes," retorts Addolorata in the play of the same name.[7] Language of power, yes, but also language of the Church. This fourth linguistic level brings into play the last reterritorialization: the spiritual one. It is not without significance that Italian is also the language of the Mass and of the important regional holidays in the different parishes, such as Notre-Dame della Consolata or Madonna della Difesa.[8] More than the language of religion, Italian is the language of the Golden Age, of union, from before the migratory Fall. The determination of the parents to have their children learn Italian in Saturday morning classes stems in large part from this.[9] Whether he wants to or not, the Italian intellectual will be forced to define himself in relation to Italian. He will do so, either in ignorance of the language or by relearning it with fervor and fascination. Language of Eden, language of Return in the manner of Hebrew for the Jews, Italian has provoked contradictory feelings of hate, love and indifference.[10]

To what use will the Italian writers put these four languages? Whereas the writers from Toronto and Vancouver orient themselves towards a reterritorialization through the use of English, the Montreal writer has more than one choice: either he goes through a reterritorialization through the use of Quebecois (the language chosen by Marco Micone in his plays), or he uses English hyperculturally by implanting a twist in the syntax with symbolic and oniric overtones. This is the case in the poetry of Mary Melfi and Antonio D'Alfonso. The poem "Babel" written by the latter, eloquently evokes the multiple linguistic juxtaposition practiced by Italians in Montreal.

> *Nativo di Montréal*
> *élevé comme Québécois*
> *forced to learn the tongue of power*
> *vivi en Mexico como alternativa*
> *figlio del sole e della campagna*
> *par les franc-parleurs aimé*
> *finding thousands like me suffering*
> *me casé y divorcié en tierra fria*
> *nipote de Guglionesi*
> *parlant politique malgré moi*
> steeled in the school of Old Aquinas
> *queriendo luchar con mis amigos latinos*
> *Dio where shall I be demain*
> *(trop vif) qué puedo saber yo*
> *spero she la terra be mine.*[11]

Dialect is from the outset rejected by the Italian writer; he clearly prefers, to all evidence, to use fragments of

Italian in his works as proof of both Italian descent and immigration.

Writing directly in Italian poses a seductive alternative for more than one second-generation writer; fantasy of the eternal Return which will blot out the pain of departure. Its implementation, in order to be successful, apparently requires a return in part to one's Italian roots (citizenship, return to the native country or even immigration) if frequent contact with Italy has not been established. The first collection of poems by Filippo Salvatore clearly illustrates this situation. Originally written in Italian, *Tufo e gramigna* was subsequently translated into English by the author himself and published in a bilingual edition with the title *Suns of Darkness*. The poem ''Bagliore di folgore'' takes note of the defeat of Italian, a language illuminated at times by a flash of ''lightning'':

> *Eroe sono*
> *eroe della sconfitta*
> *e la lingua pura che m'illumina*
> *è bagliore di folgore.*[12]

While this lightning flash may mark the defeat of Italian, it also announces its assumption. Thus stripped of any historical context linked to immigration, Italian is raised to a broader level from which everyone can draw inspiration. First and foremost, the Italians themselves. This nascent tendency is incarnated by someone like D'Alfonso: this native-born Montrealer began to write in Italian. The language of Return can thus serve as a traditional way of bringing to light the hidden aspect of cultural heritage.[13] It is still too early to tell if this trend towards Italian will produce the desired results.

In the interval, there exists an as yet unexplored avenue between Italian and dialect. Namely, the intensive use of language. This usage is a result of an increasing weakness and drying up of the language, along with an internal erosion; economy of metaphor and syntax. Thus refined, language becomes a vehicle for self-expression "capable of disorganizing its own forms and the forms of content in order to free pure content which blends into a single, highly-charged material."[14] This is the method borrowed by Kafka.

In Montreal, curiously enough, both majority languages, French and English, lend themselves to this intensive usage, but for opposite reasons. I limit myself here to a discussion of the two languages of this city since it is the example I am most familiar with. The English which the young Italian learned at school was filtered through contact with a social group often mono-ethnic and immigrant like himself. This is the process of in-breeding, a situation which has affected his way of speaking Shakespeare's language. An imperfect English, distorted and maintaining a precarious relationship to mainstream English. It is only with university attendance that this situation will be corrected.

The Quebecois spoken in Montreal has already undergone this distortion. The omnipresence of English in the vocabulary of Quebecois, plus its sheltered evolution of three centuries, bestow it with the characteristics of a minority language whose subjection was deplored by Gaston Miron at the onset of the Sixties.

> Je sais ce que je sais ceci, ma culture polluée, mon dualisme linguistique, ceci, le non-poème qui a détruit en moi jusqu'à la racine des mots français.[15]

This language of dispossession was appropriated by the Quebecois writers: some of them attempted to purge the language of Anglicisms and lexical constraints to make of it "an instrument of thought and action."[16] Others, on the contrary, claimed it in its state of semantic distortion. They tried to transform it into a language of everyday speech through *Le Cassé* by Renaud and through *Les Belles-Sœurs* by Tremblay.

However, the intensive usage of Quebecois seems to have begun with Réjean Ducharme. In his novels, he makes use of the pun and word-play to bring out the language, to make it "shout."[17] Hubert Aquin chooses a baroque and hypercultural language, through his choice of symbols, political and cultural metaphors, and empty signs which he continuously reworks.[18] But this desperate attempt quickly attained its limits. It implied an effort at "symbolic reterritorialization, based on Kabbalistic archetypes... which only accentuates its rupture with the populace and which can only end politically in Zionism and the Zionist dream."[19]

For Aquin, of course, it is not a question of Zionism, but of nationalism and "the dream of independence." By deliberately applying the commentary of the two French thinkers in regards to the turn of the century literary school of Prague, to the work of this Montreal writer, we are able to discern to what extent his style takes a route ressembling, even though a century apart, that taken by Gustave Meyrink, for example.[20] They are of the same kind. It is as if their language, desiring at any price to reterritorialize itself without being able to, flays itself, turning in, circles upon itself, within its own world, reworking the same symbols, brandishing them like flags. Without being aware of it, the allegorization of literary language had begun.

This process is a kind of slow death, centred on a schizoid inability to express itself. The French writer Michel Tournier was not mistaken when he stated that allegory is a "death myth" and that the role of the writer is precisely to prevent this deadly process.[21] The renewal of the myth is effected through the use of metaphor. To be practicable, this work with language must be interiorized, kept hidden, a secret even. To tear it away from its shadowy realm is to condemn language to a codification through allegory, and so to history and obsolescence. This explains Kafka's intense dislike of metaphor. For he was aware that this natural use of literary language was henceforth forbidden to him, since it lead inexorably to allegory.[22] To recapture the myth, he had then to proceed in reverse by eliminating all metaphor in his use of language.

For the Italian writing in French, the route chosen by Kafka (which is here borrowed by Ducharme) is without doubt the more interesting one. The Italian writer cannot evoke such a language since he has not had an objective experience of colonization. His situation is the exact opposite to that of the colonized, for immigration is none other than *reverse colonization*. It is not an accident that the route of one inversely ressembles the other, as Filippo Salvatore shows us in his play *La Fresque de Mussolini*.[23]

In contrast to the Quebecois, the immigrant intellectual is not required to go through "the painful turning in towards self" of which Miron speaks in one of his essays. For he knows from the start that he will lose both his language and his culture sooner or later. This search for identity begins with the theme of the loss of the mother country and of the conflicts between the value system of the host country as adopted by the children, and those of the country symbolized by the parents. The novelist Frank Paci of Sault-Ste-Marie has dramatized these situations in books such as *Black Madonna*.[24] This acculturation, lived in sorrow if not distress, leads to want, crisis and the void. These are the themes which occur, symptomatically, over and over in the work of Italian writers. However, this theme of the void, of confusion and helplessness has not yet found a corresponding form. *Addolorata* shows the tragic irony of this acculturation through the statements of immigrant children.

A Saint-Léonard, i a déjà eu des écoles bilingues anglaises pour les Italiens, mais ç'a pas marché. I se sont aperçus que c'est pas nécessaire d'enseigner les deux langues à l'école parce que les Italiens apprennent déjà le français dans la rue. Et la rue, pour apprendre le français, c'est pas pire que l'école. C'est la même chose pour l'italien. On n'a pas besoin de l'étudier: on a ça dans le sang. Pour nous les Italiens, l'école est presque pas utile. Tous mes amis ont lâché ça le plus vite possible. Moi j'passe pour l'intellectuelle de la gang... Je m'ennuie jamais avec mes quatre langues. J'peux parler l'anglais le lundi, le français le mardi, l'italien le mercredi, l'espagnol le jeudi. Et les quatre à la fois le vendredi. [25]

In order to explain the situation, the Italian writer must go beyond the first acculturation caused by the shock of migration and integrate the second dating from his adolescence at the beginning of the Seventies. We are dealing here with the cultural mutation of the years 1968-73, identified in its beginnings by thinkers such as Baudrillard, Lyotard and Pasolini. This upheaval in the value system, amplified by the media, was felt throughout the different classes of post-industrial society. Not only did it level out and modify lifestyles, accentuating even further the gap between the first generation and their children, but it also destabilized the relationship to language, at the very moment when the baby boom generation of the middle class was going to school. [26] This resulted in the phenomena of drop-outs and raised the coefficient of deterritorialization several degrees. Quebecois enriched itself with Parisian idioms and Anglo-American expressions inherited from rock culture. [27]

However, for the Italian, this double acculturation, brought about in a relatively short period of time, operates as a "recentering" which allows him to exploit his own shortcomings through the intensive use of language as a vehicle for self-expression. [28]

NOTES

Epigram by Claude Bertrand and Michel Morin, *Le Territoire de la culture* (Montréal: HMH Brèches, 1979).

1 Régis Debray, *Le Scribe* (Paris: Le livre de poche, 1983).

2 Gilles Deleuze and Félix Guattari, *Kafka — Pour une littérature mineure*. (Paris: Les éditions de minuit, 1975).

3 Henri Gobard, *L'Aliénation linguistique: analyse tétraglossique*. (Paris: Flammarion, 1976).

4 Marco Micone, *Gens du silence* (Montréal: Editions Québec-Amérique, 1982). See *Voiceless People* (Guernica, 1984).

5 "Mary di Michele interviewed by Joseph Pivato", *Vice Versa*, vol. 1, no. 5-6 (June, 1984), p. 22.

6 Pier Giorgio Di Cicco, ed. *Roman Candles* (Toronto: Hounslow Press, 1978), Caroline M. Di Giovanni, ed. *Italian-Canadian Voices* (Oakville: Mosaic Press, 1984), Tonino Caticchio, ed. *La poesia Italiana nel Québec* (Montréal: Centro Italiano di Cultura Popolare, 1983), and Fulvio Caccia and Antonio D'Alfonso, eds. *Quêtes: Textes d'auteurs italo-québécois* (Montréal: Guernica, 1983).

7 Marco Micone, *Addolorata* (Montréal: Guernica, 1984).

8 Throughout Canada and in particular Quebec, the Italian clergy did not have to confront the powerful hegemony of the Irish clergy as did their American colleagues. Here, the opposite was the case. Thus, the archdiocese of Montreal, through the urging of Cardinal Léger, favored the use of Italian in both liturgy and the catechism. References: Father Crespi, interviewed by Fulvio Caccia in the program series titled *The Italian Community in Quebec*, broadcast by Radio-Canada from the 6th to the 10th of June, 1983, and Stephen S. Hall, "Italian-Americans Coming Into Their Own", *The New York Times Magazine*, 15th May, 1983.

9 A large section of the second generation studied Italian in courses given by PICAI (Patronat Italien Canadien d'Assistance aux Immigrants).

10 Régine Robin, *L'Amour du Yiddish* (Paris: Les Editions du Sorbier, 1983).

11 Antonio D'Alfonso, "Babel", in *Quêtes, op. cit.*, p. 201.

12 Filippo Salvatore, *Tufo e Gramigna* (Montreal: Edizioni Simposium, 1977), p. 32. The bilingual edition is *Suns of Darkness* (Montreal: Guernica, 1980). Cf. Giovanni Di Lullo, *Il fuoco della pira* (Montreal: Edizioni Simposium, 1976).

13 This reterritorialization by the Italian outside of Italy would be of marginal interest, if there did not exist concurrently a growing number of young Quebecois who are interested in learning Italian. This outlook opens a new avenue as regards ways of perceiving a possible future for Italian as a referential language. It is tempting to imagine the contribution of a certain number of Italian writers willing to pursue the movement transmitted by Vittorini and Pavese: to lighten up Italian prose till now weighted down by rhetorical formulas. This step would ressemble the modernization of ancient Hebrew begun at the turn of the century, following its confrontation with Yiddish.

14 Deleuze and Guattari, *op. cit.*, p. 51.

15 Gaston Miron, *L'Homme rapaillé* (Montreal: Les Presses de l'Université de Montréal, 1970).

16 Georges-André Vachon, "Gaston Miron ou l'invention de la substance", *Etudes françaises* (1970), pp. 133-149.

17 Réjean Ducharme, *L'Hiver de force* (Paris: Gallimard, 1973).

18 Hubert Aquin, *Prochain épisode* (Montreal: Le Cercle de livre, 1965).

19 Deleuze and Guattari, *op. cit.*, p. 79.

20 Gustav Meyrink, *Le Golem* (Marabout: Biblio 387, 1979). The Jewish writer has always maintained a complex relationship with many languages. In reference to this, see the fascinating study by Régine Robin, *L'Amour du Yiddish* (Paris: Editions du Sorbier, 1983).

21 Michel Tournier, *Le Vent paraclet* (Paris: Gallimard, 1977),

22 Frank Kafka, *Journal* (Paris: le livre de poche, Biblio, 1982).

23 Filippo Salvatore, *La Fresque de Mussolini* (Montreal: Guernica, 1985).

24 Frank Paci, *Black Madonna* (Ottawa: Oberon Press, 1982).

25 Micone, *Addolorata, op. cit.*, p. 67.

26 This model which emerges from the young Italian Quebecois should be related to the current rise of a new generation of English Canadians in the West who speak French. Even though the two phenomena do not have the same origin, nor even the same social structure, both of them confirm new tendencies towards by-passing national languages.

27 The writer is the privileged witness of the evolution of a language. Just as Borges noted the transformation of Argentinian Spanish following the massive immigration of Italians at the end of the 19th century, it would also be of interest to note the state of the language as spoken by immigrants.

28 Other references to see: Mary Melfi, *A Bride in Three Acts* (Montreal: Guernica, 1983), Bruno Ramirez, *Les Premiers Italiens de Montréal* (Montréal: Boréal Express, 1984), Jean Blouin, "Le Silence parle Italien: Marco Micone, l'enfant terrible de la Petite Italie", *L'Actualité* (July, 1984), pp. 68-73. F. Caccia, "Les Poètes italo-montréalais: Sous le signe du Phénix", *Canadian Literature* 106 (1985).

JOSEPH PIVATO

A Literature of Exile:
Italian Language Writing
in Canada

Perch'io no spero di tonar giammai,
ballatetta, in Toscana,
va' tu, leggera e piana,
dritt' a la donna mia,
che per la sua cortesia
ti farà molto onore.

Guido Cavalcanti

In both Italian literature and history the theme of exile
has been very prominent. From Roman times Italians
have always been leaving home, trying to return home,
or, like Vergil's *pius Aeneas*, trying to find a new home.
Both Cavalcanti and Dante died in exile away from
Florence. In the *Divina Commedia* the feelings of nostalgia for home and the sense of exile are very strong. In
Manzoni's *I promessi sposi* the goal of Renzo and Lucia
is to return home safely in order to get married. The displacement of people during two world wars has resulted
in many novels on exile and alienation. The works of
Moravia, Bassani and others come to mind.

Italian-Canadian writers are continuing in this tradition of exploring the state of exile. There are three
groups of Italian-Canadian writers: the older generation
writing mostly in Italian, the younger generation writing
in English and another group writing mostly in French.[1]

This paper shall focus on Italian writers publishing
in Italian, but also refer to works in English and French.

When we consider the concept of exile we are not
restricted to the concrete idea of physical displacement,

or legal separation. We must also explore the abstract, the psychological significance, the sense of home, the feeling of belonging. The state of exile is the absence of a sense of home. A number of Italian-Canadian writers are dealing with this theme in Canada. The concept of exile for Italians has various complex aspects that a number of writers are placing under creative scrutiny. In this brief study we shall point out some of the preoccupations with the sense of exile that is demonstrated in the work of: Mario Duliani, Romano Perticarini, Maria Ardizzi, Antonio F. Corea, Matilde Torres, Giovanni di Lullo, Gianni Grohovaz, Elena Albani and others.

The first Italians to come to Canada did not look upon it as a possible home. Giovanni Caboto and his sons regarded it as an obstacle on the way to Asia. In his history, *Gli Italiani in Canada*, Guglielmo Vangelisti writes:

> Giovanni Caboto era nella convinzione d'avere raggiunto le coste dell'Asia e si teneva sicuro di potere arrivare fino al Giappone... Per questo is sforzava di trovare un passaggio che lo menasse al di là delle terre scoperte da lui; ma tutto inutile. [2]

In 1653 Frencesco Bressani published his *Breve Relatione* recounting his experiences in, and his impressions of Canada. This Italian Jesuit missionary lived and worked in this country and suffered persecution at the hands of the Indians. Bressani is a paradox: despite his heroic experiences in Canada he seems to have formed no particular attachment to the country; nevertheless, he considers it important to write his *Breve Relatione* in Italian for an Italian audience. His account is objective, cold, detached. Even in a passing comparison with Italy we get the impression that *la Nuova Francia* could never be home for European people. He says

[Il paese] partecipa le qualità delle due estreme, essendovi l'Inverno gran freddi, altissime nevi, e durissimi ghiacci; e l'Estate caldi non minori di quelli dell' Italia.[3]

With mass Italian immigration, these attitudes seem to change.

In 1946, Mario Duliani published an autobiographical novel about his experiences in an internment camp during the war. Duliani, who had come to Montreal in 1936 to work as a French journalist for *La Presse*, wants us to believe that Canada is his new home. His book, *Città senza donne*, is in part a defence of the way Italians in Canada were treated during the war. Despite Duliani's convictions and the sincerity of his arguments we cannot help but feel uneasy about the situation. Is this internment the way one is treated at home?

At many points in the book Duliani admits to the spiritual deterioration of the internees. From the Italian edition of this book we read:

Non ho mai udito qualcosa di più patetico di queste parole dettemi da un italiano giunto al Canada allorchè era ancora un bambino, naturalizzato da trentasei anni e che — a forza di lavoro — è riuscito a crearsi una situazione invidiabile. — La privazione della mia libertà, l'allontanamento dalla mia famiglia, la perdita del mio tempo e del mio denaro: tutto ciò non conta più! Lo accetto senza lagnarmi... Ma quello che mi è insopportabile è l'idea che mia moglie, canadese, ed i miei figli, canadesi, anch'essi, possano sospettarmi di avere tradito il *nostro* paese![4]

Il nostro paese is Canada. This man considers himself Canadian, but to others, even his family he is a foreigner, an enemy alien.

Internment is a form of physical separation that can result in social isolation and psychological alienation. It is a form of exile. Duliani's novel is about men surviving this exile. The title, *Città senza donne*, implies this state where natural social interaction is absent. Despite Duliani's apologetic intentions the novel is a kind of laboratory study of some of the conditions of exile found in later works of Italian-Canadian literature. Over and over again we find similar sentiments: separation from family and friends, guilt or regret at leaving home, nostalgia for an ideal past, inability to communicate because of language problems and loss of identity.

When we turn to Vancouver poet, Romano Perticarini, we find a sense of exile expressed by elegies over the loss of childhood, regret, guilt and death. In his bilingual collection, *Quelli della Fionda*, Perticarini shows that the word, *emigrante*, has special associations for the Italian immigrant. This is dramatically captured in the poem entitled "Emigrante":

> *e noi con i primi esuli,*
> *stanchi d'un pane nero,*
> *stanchi di correre, di cercare,*
> *e nelle piatte città d'acciaio*
> *ci lasciammo vincere, esiliare.*[5]

Like the word, *emigrante, esilio* carries a wealth of meaning for an Italian. The mythology around these words has become part of Italian folklore.[6] These myths show a paradoxical mixture of good and evil elements. The new land is abundant; the immigrant may prosper, but at what cost, his attachment to the homeland? Perticarini writes:

> *È questo immenso paese*
> *generoso come mia madre,*
> *che vorrei amare,*
> *e che non amo ancora* (p. 62).

The poet has several elegies for his mother in this collection. Thus, when he compares Canada to his mother it is significant. The loss of parents, the separation from family may be compensated for by a new mother, Canada. But the speaker tells us *che vorrei amare/e che non amo ancora*. The gap is not easily filled. There is great guilt at leaving. The poet is literally haunted by memories and regrets of childhood. Why can he not love Canada? The poet goes on to tell us:

> *sono schiavo delle voci*
> *che ricordano mio padre,*
> *mia madre, i fratelli,*
> *il sussurro della fonte,*
> *il pianto mio fanciullo* (p. 62).

Canada is not home for this poet. Home is the ideal past in Italy. The Italian childhood becomes the central myth in the book. As the title, *Quelli della Fionda*, indicates the freedom of childhood colours the entire collection. The title poem ends with the declaration, *Amici credetimi!/Tornerei indietro...* For Perticarni exile from Italy is also separation from an idyllic childhood. The new land then is the harsh reality of growing up, of facing disillusionment.

Maria Ardizzi's realistic novel, *Made in Italy*, would appear to be in contrast to Perticarini's apparent poetic sentiments. Ardizzi's heroine, Nora Moratti, is an old woman who has been toughened by her immigrant experiences. As the novel opens she has buried a husband and by the end, she buries two sons. Yet for all her hardness, for all her individuality Nora remains an immigrant mother, affected by alienation, a victim of exile.[7]

Nora's view of the world is an ingenuous one. Hers

is a naiveté shared by many Italians; because of sheer lack of experience, adaptation to other parts of the world appears easy. Nora explains the immigrant myth, or as she calls it, *l'idea dell' estero*:

> Nella mia infanzia, ho sempre sentito di persone partite per diversi luoghi del mondo; ho veduto quelle persone tornare e ripartire. Portavano con sé aria di benessere e di raggiunta stabilità... Quando l'idea dell'estero... venne ad interrompere il fluire delle nostre vite, accettai il mutamento con la sorpresa, e la curiosità, con cui lo avevano accettato altri. La convinzione che ogni parte del mondo potesse essere anche mia, e che altrove le persone non sarebbero migliori o peggiori di quelle conosciute, non mi diede l'idea della perdita e del distaco (p. 15).

Only after her physical displacement to Canada does Nora realize that her view of the world is unrealistic. Nevertheless, Nora is obliged to cling to the ideal notions of the immigrant myth:

> Il significato della parola emigrante mi ha... colpita solo dopo aver emigrato: e mi ha colpita per le implicazioni che balzano... solo quando sei emigrante (p. 15).

> Ed anche quando ho scoperto che il mondo non appartiene affatto a tutti, e che le disuguaglianze non sono soltanto nel linguaggio, ho conservato la mia convinzione, la sola forza che mi permettesse di sentirmi ovunque a casa mia (p. 16).

It is this illusion of "sentirmi a casa mia," that permits Nora to survive the alienation of her condition. Nora tries to avoid coming to terms with harsh external reality by creating an internal subjective reality. Like Perticarini's poems it is the myth, "nella mia infanzia," the childhood point of view that is paramount.

In contrast to individualistic perspectives that Nora wishes to maintain we are also given many examples of the vicissitudes of exile.

Solo più tardi, molto più tardi, dovevo... scoprire l'anonimità della livertà e l'altezza tragica dei nostri destini. Ma, a quel punto ero sganciata dal tempo, dai luoghi, dalla nostra stessa condizione. Emigranti? Une parola che non ci definiva affato. La gabbia nella quale ci movevamo si andava facendo sempre più stretta, lasciava appena un pertugio per guardare il cielo (p. 93).

The images of exile here are powerful and paradoxical: exile is free of points of reference: "sganciata dal tempo, dai luoghi, dalla nostra stessa condizione," but also "una gabbia stretta."

The ultimate condition of exile in *Made in Italy* is the inability to communicate. Ardizzi has represented this *gabbia stretta* in several forms of isolation that are related to the immigrant status. The author uses the language barrier, the marriage disintegration, the generation gap and physical breakdown as metaphors for alienation.

Per la prima volta, una sorta di paura mi chiudeva la bocca; se parlavo, la voce mi usciva in un sussurro. Il mio linguaggio si ergeva come un muro tra me ed il mondo intorno. Allora, di nascosto, cominciai a rovistare tra i libri di Andrea e di Matteo; imparavo le parole di uso quotidiano con la segretezza e la cautela di chi commette un furto (p. 95).

Nora and her husband, Vanni, have not had a verbal exchange for many years. His financial success in Canada has simply made them move further apart. The three grown up children no longer talk to their mother, nor do they visit the old woman. This breakdown in the generations of the family is aggravated by the life experience of Nora in Italy, that separates her from her children and grandchildren. Nora does not understand them, nor they her. Nora is closed off from the world by all these aspects that contribute to her incommunicability. Like Marco Micone's *Gens du silence*, reality for

Nora is the inarticulate, the silent, a symbol of the Italian condition in Canada.

Though a strong woman, Nora is ultimately unable to cope with the external reality, unable to reconcile the subjective and the objective world, unable to accept her son's death. She has a breakdown that leaves her paralyzed so that she can no longer speak, though she can hear and comprehend. Ironically her family think that all her senses are gone. Internal reality finally conforms to the external condition of exile. Her earlier condition of separation, alienation and inability to communicate are epitomized at the end of the novel by Nora's paralysis. The wheel chair becomes a symbol, like the *gabbia*, of immigrant exile. Nora as a silent observer of life, rather than a participant in life, speaks to the Italian immigrants she represents.

The recurrence of characters with physical handicaps suggests that it is a metaphor for the immigrant condition. In F.G. Paci's *The Italians*, Alberto, the father, loses an arm and in *The Father* Stephen Mancuso has a withered hand. Both mother and daughter in *Black Madonna* deform their bodies.

In the autobiographical narrative, *La dottoressa di Cappadocia*, Matilde Torres recalls the events in her early medical career and her coming to Canada. As a woman doctor she is no ordinary immigrant yet the feeling of homelessness is no less acute:

> L'emigrante sta alla patria come l'adolescente alla vita; entrambi sono apolidi. E come gli adolescenti hanno perduto i privilegi dell'infanzia, senza aver ancora guadagnato quelli degli adulti, così l'emigrante spesso perde la patria, senza riuscire ad integrarsi nel paese in cui si stabilisce. E se, dono un periodo di tempo, l'emigrante decide di rimpatriare definitivamente, si accorge che l'Italia non è più quella che aveva lasciato e nel cui ricordo era vissuto durante gli anni di permanenza all'estaro. Si sente a disagio, uno straniero nella sua patria.[8]

You cannot go home again, Giovanni di Lullo explains in his poem, "1975: Il Ritorno," that ends: *Tutto ho lasciato ma non il ricordo.*[9] The memory of childhood, the past, traps the immigrant in a kind of never-never-land; he cannot go back, but as Torres points out, he does not belong to the present either.

The disorientation of the immigrant is treated with irony and humour by Antonio Filippo Corea in *I passi.* In contrast to the lighter poems, "One Way," and "Notte canabra," Corea explores sadder moments in "Calabria,"

> *Ritorni inaspettata*
> *nei ricordi,*
> *con gli occhi seri*
> *d'una madre in pena;*
> *chiedi della promessa*
> *fatta allora,*
> *"Non posso ancor tornar"*
> *io dico, "spera."*[10]

In his second collection of poems, *Il mio quaderno di novembre*, Perticarini continues his examination of the meaning of *emigrante* in a poem by that name:

> *Rimbocca le maniche*
> *ricuci la voglia di ritornare*
> *e lotta per la tua strada*
> *io ho lottato anche...*[11]

In the mythic novel of Gianni Grohovaz, *La strada bianca*, the central metaphor is *la strada*, the white road, the open road, the road of snow, the wake of the immigrant ship, the unmarked road of no return.[12] One of the many immigrant writers who has combined journalism with imaginative work, Gianni Grohovaz has devoted several poems in his collections, *Per ricordar le cose che rocordo* and *Parole, parole e granelli di sabbia*, to the problem of memory and returning home.[13] Born in Fiume, now part of Yugoslavia, Grohovaz can never return home, not even for a visit.

Many Italian writers and journalists have published creative work but it often does not deal with immigrants or the problems of adjustment to a new country. The novels of Camillo Carli seem international in their perspective as do the many stories of Gianni Bartocci. The stories of Dino Fruchi deal with Toscana while those of Michele Pirone deal with Napoli. In his anthology, *La poesia italiana nel Quebec*, Tonino Caticchio was able to gather much material on immigrant themes of exile and dislocation. Many of the writers in this collection look back with regret: Corrado Mastropasqua to Napoli and Ermanno La Riccia to the exile of the immigrant.[14]

The sense of homelessness is not restricted to the immigrant parents — the generation of Perticarini, Grohovaz and Ardizzi. It is also evident in their children, who must deal with the duality of their life experience in an Italian home and the necessity of functioning in an English society. (Those in French-Canada have peculiar forms of adaptation to the situation in Quebec.) These children are now writing and publishing.

For the first time the Italian community in Canada has a large generation of university educated young people. The Italian writers I am referring to now come from this mobile and articulate generation. All are university educated and in their twenties and thirties. Frank Paci's novels, *The Italians, Black Madonna*, the short stories of C.D. Minni, the poetry of Pier Giorgio Di Cicco, Filippo Salvatore, Mary di Michele, and Alexandre Amprimoz are primarily products of the 1970's and 1980's and thus reflect the experiences of an affluent urban society. While this generation may now be following professional careers they remember that many of their fathers began their new life in Canada as labourers and many of their mothers worked in factories. Since they are still close to this background of labour they are well aware of the gaps between former hardships and present affluence. The struggle is often recalled in their works, the price often questioned.

What is also important is that there is an audience for this work. These young writers are speaking for the Italian community, representing their experiences. The examination of the problem of exile in these writers becomes a search for the nature of the duality of the Italian-Canadian experience. Some people appear to be comfortable with this duality. Mario, the little Italian boy in Dino Minni's short story, "Details from the Canadian Mosaic," discovers this duality one day:

> He did not know at what point he had become Mike. One day looking for a suitable translation of his name and finding none, he decided that Mike was closest. By the end of the summer, he was Mario at home and Mike in the streets.[15]

On the other hand some people are disturbed by this sense of otherness, this confused identity. In Frank Paci's novel, *The Italians*, Lorianna feels only guilt and complains to her father: "But I'm the one who desn't know whether she's Italian or Canadian..." Her brother, Bill, tries to escape his Italian side through hockey:

> He felt somewhat alien in a house filled with Italians. He was more at home on an ice surface. There his rhythm of freedom was unquestionable... It seemed to make him less Italian.[16]

One of the paradoxes of Paci's second novel, *Black Madonna*, is that the main character, Assunta, the black madonna, remains an unknown character although the focus of considerable attention. We always see Assunta from the outside, either through the eyes of her son,

Joey, or her daughter, Marie. We are never permitted inside this Italian mother; she remains a mystery. Since she realistically represents that silent first generation of immigrants, Assunta speaks no English and is not very verbal in Italian either. She is the archetypal Italian mother caught in the *gabbia* of immigrant exile.[17]

Within the story itself, Assunta, remains alienated from others. Adamo, her husband, originally married her by proxy, not having previously met her. He accepted her peculiar old fashioned ways but never understood her. To her children she remains a puzzle to the end. They learn to appreciate Assunta but never to know her better.

Upon coming to Canada Assunta recognized and accepted her state of exile as an Italian woman. She talks about returning to Italy but remains dedicated to her family. Paradoxically by accepting her exile Assunta also accepted her new country. It will take many years of tribulation for her children to achieve Assunta's simple balance between old and new worlds. In the character of Assunta, Paci has interwoven that sense of fate that we find in so many immigrants of the older generation; action transcends the temporal realm.

The dominant theme in the *Black Madonna* is the exile of the immigrant experience. All three major characters demonstrate aspects of this exile, from Assunta's locked *baule* to Marie's escape to a university education. Only after Assunta dies do Marie and her brother begin to reconsider the nature of the Italian-Canadian duality.[18]

The ultimate physical separation is death. Italian-Canadian literature seems preoccupied with death. Are there Italian ghosts in Canada? For Pier Giorgio Di Cicco it is this sense of the past that helps him to overcome the profound sense of exile. Di Cicco's concern with death is seen in his poem, "Donna italiana," which recalls Etruscan ancestors, spirits that are present for him even in Canada. In "Nostagia" Di Cicco eulogizes his dead father:

> Under a few cold lilies, my father dreams
> cicadas in Vallemaio. I am sure of it.
> He left me that, and a poem that is only a
> dream of cicadas; the brown glove widens
> on the dry december earth.
> I am a little marvellous, with the sunken
> heart of exiles.[19]

For Maria Ardizzi exile is overtaken by an act of will. When Nora's husband, Vanni, died suddenly while on a trip to Italy she had to return to her home town for the first time to make funeral arrangements. Speaking to Vanni's body for the last time Nora says:

> Sei tornato a morire qui... L'avresti mai creduto? Io non potrò tornare a morire qui invece... e non perché non voglia. Semplicemente perché tra me e questi luoghi s'é spezzato il Lilo... Riconosco i luoghi, ma i luoghi non riconoscono me... I miei luoghi sono rimasti intatti solo nella fantasia, e non posso possederli che con la fantasia... Vuoi saperlo? Non ho piú un vero posto. Non appartengo a nessun luogo... ed appartengo a tutti i luoghi... (p. 125).

The only way to transcend the exile is by means of *la fantasia*, a courageous act of the imagination. Italian-Canadian writers are making significant contributions to the spiritual life of immigrants and the children of immigrants.

Of the many Italian-language writers publishing in Canada the ones that are most clearly concerned with exile are the women writers. An early example is Elena Albani's *Canada: mia seconda patria*, a novel that deals with an Italian woman's move to Canada in 1940. Claudia is left in Montreal with her little daughter, Anna, while her husband, Michele, returns to Ferrara to straighten out business affairs. In June of that year Canada declares war on Italy. Claudia loses contact with her husband back in Italy. During these difficult war months she becomes involved with a young Canadian, Bruce Ansley. With the eventual end of the war Claudia ends her exile in a foreign city and learns about her husband.[20]

In Tonino Caticchio's *La poesia italiana nel Quebec*, there are several women poets: Giovanna De Masi, Marà Di Lalla, Concetta Kosseim, Alda Viero and Annita Pagliero. In the anthology, *Quêtes: Textes d'auteurs italo-québécois*, edited by Fulvio Caccia and Antonio D'Alfonso only two women are included, Mary Melfi and Carole Fioramore-David.[21] In western Canada the female presence is represented by Caterina Edwards with, *The Lion's Mouth*, a novel that explores the search for identity of a young women from the second generation of Italians.[22]

With the publication of her second novel, *Il sapore agro della mia terra*, Maria Ardizzi has emerged as a strong voice in Italian immigrant writing both in Canada and Italy.[23] The two worlds that are explored in this realistic novel are familiar to generations of Italian immigrants; the poverty of the Italian *contadini* is contrasted against the affluence of the new life in Canadian cities. *Il sapore agro della mia terra*, as the title suggests, deals with the suffering that a family of *contadini* endures before, during and after World War II. The two settings for the story of the Valtoni family, the Marghera country of the Abruzzi region and the Toronto of the 1950's construction boom, could not be further apart. Yet the two are brought together by the dreams of two people. The oldest daughter, Sara Valtoni, longs to improve her lot and to leave La Marghera. From Canada, the old uncle, Joe Valtoni, longs to have a family and invites them to join him and share his success.

The first part of the story takes place in the arid hills of the Abruzzi. The Valtoni are tenant farmers who are born and die on land they will never own. They suffer the loss of men during the war, the German occupation, the partisans and the death of family members. The Valtoni barely survive the war only to find that their land has been sold to new landlords. *L'atto di richiamo* of Joe Valtoni rescues the family from their hopeless poverty and subservience to landlords.

The irony of the Valtoni's emigration to Canada is the conflict in motivation between the men and the women. Ardizzi's treatment of this on-going conflict is the most striking element in the novel. The character of Sara Valtoni is memorable as an image of the new woman in immigrant literature. In contrast to Teresa and Lisa, Sara sees the move to Canada as an opportunity to break away from the repressive old ways of superstition, male dominance, harsh farm work and the submissive roles of wife and mother.

> Io voglio andare a scuola. Voglio conoscere il mondo fuori della Marghera. Lo sai quante città ci sono...? (p. 11)

Joe Valtoni and Stefano see the move as a way of maintaining the old ways. For Joe the arrival of his Italian relatives fulfills his dream of having an Italian family in Canada. Though in North America for many years Joe still retains the old values, the mythical patriarchal family. These values which resulted in the estrangement of his Canadian-born wife later cause conflict within the family. Joe maintains that, "La nostra vocazione e la famiglia," (p. 232) but his authoritarian interference drives the family apart.

Sara is as strong willed as her uncle Joe and is determined to be independent of men. She studies privately and struggles to go on in school. Her rejection of traditional roles does not lead to happiness or a better sense of self worth. Sara seems forever caught in the immigrant duality.

> Io, chi sono? ... sono un'emigrante. Non sarò mai separata dal mio vecchio mondo, ho pensato. Potrò sottrarmi al nuovo mondo? Rimarrò qualcosa di mezzo, che non sta né da una parte né dall'altra? (p. 175)

Sara makes a return trip to Marghera only to find that her love for Don Fabiano is impossible since he has returned to his ministry.

Ardizzi uses passages from Sara's diary to reveal a troubled and introspective woman. In contrast to Paci's *Black Madonna* Sara reminds us of Nora Moratti in *Made in Italy* and Bianca in *The Lion's Mouth* by Caterina Edwards. This second novel in Ardizzi's triology, *Il ciclo degli emigranti*, is stylistically different from the first work, *Made in Italy*. The narrative is chronological except for Sara's short diary passages.

There is a significant shift in *Il sapore agro della mia terra*. More than other Italian-language works produced in Canada it regards this country no longer as the land of exile but as the promised land that has rescued the family from poverty. This clear perception of the new home in Canada is contributing to the new sense of belonging and a new awareness of an Italian-Canadian identity. Prairie novelist, Robert Kroetsch, explains the importance of writing about one's background: "In a sense, we haven't got an identity until somebody tells our story. The fiction makes us real." This is the function of these Italian-Canadian writers — to make us real. It is appropriate to end this examination of exile with Ardizzi's *Il sapore agro della mia terra*, a work that points to positive directions in the future of Italian writing in Canada.[24]

NOTES

1 When we place Italian-Canadian writing, or Canadian Literature, in the larger
context of world literature we find that the thesis of Margaret Atwood developed
from the theme of survival and that of John Moss based on isolation cannot be
identified as peculiarly Canadian any more than other themes.

2 Guglielmo Vangelisti, *Gli Italiani in Canada* (Montreal: Chiesa Italiana di N.S.
Della Difesa, 1956), p. 16.

3 Francesco Bressani, *Breve Relazione* in *The Jesuit Relations and Allied Documents*, ed. Reuben Gold Thwaites (Cleveland: Barrow Brothers, 1899), Vol. 38,
p. .

4 Mario Duliani, *Città senza donne* (Montreal: Gustavo D'Errico editore, 1946),
pp. 64-65. See also the French edition, *La Ville sans femmes* (Montréal: Société
des éditions Pascal, 1945).

5 Romano Perticarini, *Quelli della fionda/The Sling-shot Kids* (Vancouver: Azzi
Publishing, 1981), p. 90. All other quotations from this edition are given in the
text.

6 The prominence of the immigrant experience in Italian folklore is evident in the
number of songs devoted to this topic. Some examples are: "Canto dell'emigrante," "Vusto venir in Merica," "Tornerai," "La porti un bacione a
Firenze." Cf. Ann Cornelisen, *Women of the Shadows: The Women and Mothers of Southern Italy*. (Boston: Little, Brown & Co., 1976).

7 Maria J. Ardizzi, *Made in Italy* (Toronto: Toma Publishing, 1982). Page references to this edition are given in the text. The English language edition has the
same title and publisher.

8 Matilde Torres, *La dottoressa di Cappadocia* (Roma: Edizioni delle Urbe, 1982),
p. 82.

9 Giovanni di Lullo, *Il fuoco della pira* (Montreal: Edizioni Simposium, 1976),
p. 54.

10 Antonio Filippo Corea, *I passi* (Cosenza: Rubbettino editore, 1981), p. 31.

11 Romano Perticarini, *Il mio quaderno di Novembre* (Vancouver: Scala Publishing, 1981), p. 32.

12 Gianni Grohovaz, *La strada bianca*. Only parts of this unfinished work have
been published in Toronto.

13 *Per ricordar le cose che ricordo* (Toronto: Dufferin Press, 1974) and *Parole,
parole e granelli di sabbia* (Toronto, 1980) should be compared to Grohovaz'
collection of short essays, *E con rispetto parlando...* (Toronto, 1983)

14 Tonino Caticchio, *La poesia italiana nel Quebec* (Montréal: Centro Italiano di
Cultura Popolare, 1983). Cf. Filippo Salvatore, *Tufo e gramigna* (Montreal:
Edizioni Simposium, 1977).

15 C.D. Minni, "Details from the Canadian Mosaic," in *Other Selves* (Montreal:
Guernica, 1985).

16 F.G. Paci, *The Italians* (Scarborough: Signet, 1980), p. 23.

17 F.G. Paci, *Black Madonna* (Ottawa: Oberon Press, 1982).

18 In Paci's *The Father* (Ottawa: Oberon Press, 1984) the death of the father, Oreste, seems necessary before the two sons can begin to re-evaluate their lives and to see the value of their father.

19 Pier Giorgio Di Cicco, *The Tough Romance* (Toronto: McClelland and Stewart, 1979), p. 48.

20 Elena Albani, *Canada: mia seconda patria* (Bologna: Edizioni Sirio, 1958).

21 Fulvio Caccia et Antonio D'Alfonso, eds. *Quêtes: Textes d'auteurs italo-québécois* (Montréal: Guernica, 1983).

22 Caterina Edwards, *The Lion's Mouth* (Edmonton: NeWest Press, 1982).

23 Maria J. Ardizzi, *Il sapore agro della mia terra* (Toronto: Toma Publishing, 1984). All page references from this edition are given in the text.

24 For the names and titles of the many Italian language writers in Canada see the bibliography at the end of this volume.

FILIPPO SALVATORE

The Italian Writers of Quebec:
Language, Culture and Politics

Translated by David Homel

I

Quebec in the 1980s: A Host of Interpretations

Pierre Trudeau's resignation as prime minister marked the end of an era. With his departure, the problems raised in *Cité Libre*, the journal that set down the parameters of political and cultural debate in the 1960s and 1970s, were taken off the agenda. Thinkers like Trudeau, Vadeboncœur and Pelletier had expressed the need for social equality and moral respect in dealing as equal partners with English Canada.

However, their voices could not be heard until the end of Maurice Duplessis' reign in the late 1950s. At the beginning of the following decade, a most important phenomenon occured in Quebec society: the burst of energy of what was to be called the *Quiet Revolution*. The Quiet Revolution brought about profound change in the exercise of political power. Jean Lesage and his Liberal, French-speaking technocrats destroyed the myth of French-Canadian incompetence in business and technology. The nationalization of Hydro-Québec and its subsequent financial success were seen as striking proof of their ability.

In my opinion, the most important element in this evolution was the break-up of the Church's power and the rise of lay culture. Singer-songwriters, known as *chansonniers*, such as Félix Leclerc, Gilles Vigneault and Pauline Julien were the popular spokespersons of this new concept of culture. In this Vigneault song, the Duplessis era is seen as the time of lost time:

> *Il n'y a plus de temps à perdre*
> *Il n'y a que du temps perdu*
> *Touche mes mains calme mes lèvres*
> *Couche tes pieds tout près des miens*
> *Marche et marche et neige au loin*
> *Cherche et cherche on a perdu Amour*
> *Il n'y a plus de temps à perdre*
> *Il n'y a que du temps perdu.*[1]

These artists sung the desire for personal and collective freedom and the dream of a new society. Meanwhile, Gaston Miron was publishing his poems; the Quebecois was no longer to be *l'homme rapaillé*, living the agonized life; instead, he was to become a companion of the Americas, to express the dream and — more than that — the right to the French fact in North America. Quebec was to be the homeland, the privileged locus where this reality would not be content with survival, but would flower. As Miron wrote:

> *Fragment de la vallée*
>
> *Pays de jointures et de fractures*
> *vallée de l'Archambault*
> *étroite comme les hanches d'une femme maigre*
>
> *diamantaire clarté*
> *les échos comme des oiseaux cachés.*[2]

I am limiting my discussion to Miron because, in my view, he best represents the intellectual movement that preached the reappropriation of a living space where the French language was to hold sway. Quebec was to dream and love, eat, work and die in French:

Hommes
l'Histoire ne sera peut-être plus
retenez les noms des génocides
pour qu'en votre temps vous n'ayez pas les vôtres
hommes
il faut tuer la mort qui sur nous s'abat
et ceci appelle l'insurrection de la poésie. [3]

In general, the new generation of intellectuals in 1960s French Canada, a place increasingly known as *Québec*, were expressing the romantic dream of the artist who plays a didactic role in society.

What struck me most at the time (I had just arrived in Canada) was the link between culture and politics. It was as if the Risorgimento was being born anew in a Canadian context. Indeed, in my opinion, the Quiet Revolution was for French Canada a sort of spiritual renaissance created and expressed by the intellectuals: it was a time when literary and political involvement were inseparable.

The affirmation of the French fact was not without incident. Two events prove this: the confrontation between Francophones and Italian immigrants in Saint-Léonard in 1968 over Bill 63 that again allowed students to choose which language they wanted to be educated in, and, of course, the October Crisis in 1970.

The October Crisis expressed French Canadians' collective schizophrenia. A Francophone, Pierre Trudeau, invoked the War Measures Act and imprisoned other Francophones in defense of federalism. Meanwhile, other Francophones, separatists, killed another Francophone, the Liberal minister Pierre Laporte. Gratien Gélinas has put this schizophrenia into play form in *Hier les enfants dansaient*. Pierre Gravel, the father, fights with his sons:

GRAVEL: Le séparatisme, je n'y crois pas. C'est clair et net. A mon avis, ce serait une bêtise innomable. Et une catastrophe qui plongerait la province dans une misère dont on ne verrait jamais la fin.[4]

Two concepts of Quebec's role and position, incarnated by Trudeau and René Lévesque, were in open conflict. Strangely enough, the Quebecois behaviour at the polls continued to be schizophrenic: allegiance to Trudeau on one hand, with growing sympathy for Lévesque's *Parti Québécois* and his idea of sovereignty-association on the other. The 1970s confirmed the innovative cultural dimension of the Quiet Revolution of the 1960s. It had become completely normal, if not obligatory, for a Quebec intellectual to be nationalist and for independence. Cultural movements were channeled into nationalist political applications, and the P.Q. was able to count on the combined brain power of the Quebec intelligentsia:

Mon pays ce n'est pas un pays c'est l'envers
D'un pays qui n'était ni pays ni patrie
Ma chanson ce n'est pas ma chanson c'est ma vie
C'est pour toi que je veux posséder mes hivers...[5]

Toward the mid-1970s, the links between intellectuals and politics became inextricable. The high point of this osmosis came on November 15, 1976, when Lévesque's Parti Québécois won the election. During its first mandate, the osmosis continued, and what occured was a sort of game of mirrors between the P.Q. government and the pro-independence intelligentsia. The government needed to have the historical legitimacy of sovereignty proven by academic studies. Thanks to a policy of generous grants, the government was able to use the brain power of a large number of academics. A proliferation of historical, sociological, statistical and demographic studies appeared, demonstrating the solid foundation of the P.Q. government's cultural and linguistic policies.

This phenomenon reached its peak in 1980, at the time of the Referendum on sovereignty-association. Despite the active participation of artists and thinkers on the "Yes" side, the majority of voters in Quebec voted "No". The result gave rise to varying interpretations. Through Byzantine calculations, some sociologists attempted to show that the majority of "real" Quebecois had voted Yes and, indirectly, the negative results could be attributed to the "others" — that 20% of the Quebec population with different ethnic origins. François A. Angers went as far as suggesting in an analysis published in *Le Devoir* that the right to vote in the Referendum should have been limited to people of French-Canadian ancestry, since the others could not understand the true dimension of the debate.

Among nationalists, certain extremist positions bordered on racism. After the shock of the Referendum defeat, the intellectuals were forced to reevaluate their position toward P.Q. goals. Some remained faithful and began a public polemic with Trudeau, who accused them of being blindly obedient to a political party. But in general, there was a demobilization of energies and the honeymoon between intellectuals and political power cooled, especially when the P.Q., reelected and its hand forced by the recession, struck hard against those sectors of the public service and para-public organizations that had been the backbone of its electoral support.

This historical sketch has no pretensions toward being exhaustive; its purpose is to set the current scene in cultural issues. One thing seems clear: among young Quebec thinkers, the interest in the cultural nationalism of the preceding generation is so mitigated as to be nonexistent. The poet Philippe Haeck wrote:

Je pense à celle qui dit: «Nul peuple ne fut si profondément iconoclaste envers sa propre image.» Je pense à, je rêve à, je lis, j'écris, il y a de la musique, de la douceur, une maison confortable. Au milieu d'un monde qui se défait, sépare, j'ai un jardin où les lois sont inversées: là dans cet espace rare le monde est lié liant, on partage on tendresse on silence on converse, les enfants jouent à n'importe quel âge.[6]

No longer is the collective vision predominant; its place has been usurped by individual problems. Consider the work of Claude Beausoleil or Philippe Haeck, two of the most interesting voices of the young generation. For Claude Beausoleil the artist no longer plays the political role:

> ... il y aurait la fiction il y aurait la critique
> et le jeu de mots marquant le sens il y aurait
> l'inscription et la réception ce qui
> du livre au lecteur est englouti quelque
> part dans la pratique du lu ce champ d'échanges
> de doutes et de certitudes il y aurait le temps
> qui traverse les œuvres il y aurait le projet et
> ses formes l'infusion des angles la
> trembante imagination il y aurait tout cela
> qui nous touche ou nous hante nous transforme ou
> nous sollicite des livres comme des hasards
> concrets des chutes du sens sur le papier blanc
> des éclaircissements des montagnes des
> intentions des voix des connivences des goûts
> des directions il y aurait la passion de tout
> déchiffrer.[7]

Elsewhere, a new theme is developing among women writers who are not necessarily more *indépendantistes* than feminist. In passing, we should note that even the singers have rethought their direction and have broken the game of mirrors with the P.Q. that, even in their opinion, has become a government like all the rest.

Despite this distance-taking and a growing cultural reality formed by Quebec's heterogeneous character, the following questions remain: will dormant Quebec nationalism awake for the next elections? Will the patriotic rumblings of the Société Saint-Jean-Baptiste and the P.Q. succeed in reawakening nationalism? And, more importantly, will the new intellectuals be seduced by the collective dream of independence? I think not, and I base my opinion of the emergence of a new and varied discourse among minority groups.

The 1981 Canadian Constitution recognizes English and French as official languages, without neglecting the country's multicultural character. We must decide on the meaning multiculturalism has, especially if we are to understand this country's changing human landscape. By the end of the 1980s, one half, if not more, of Canadians will be of an ethnic origin other than French or English. It follows that the country's culture will express its demographic make-up.

Should we ask, as the playwright Marco Micone does, whether that will change?

> Dans quarante ans, on sera encore immigrants. *Sempre*. C'est pas les années qu'on reste ici qui font qu'on est immigrants ou non, c'est la façon qu'on vit. Dans un pays où les riches et les patrons mènent le gouvernement par le bout du nez, tous les pauvres, tous les ouvriers sont des immigrants, même s'ils s'appellent Tremblay ou Smith. Si c'est pas nous autres les ouvriers qui prenons les décisions, on n'aura jamais de pays. C'est pour ça qu'on est tous des immigrants. Penses-tu que ceux qui prennent les décisions à notre place pensent à nos intérêts? Regarde autour de toi: de tous ceux qui sont venus d'Italie, y en a un sur mille qui a réussi. Et pas toujours honnêtement. Les plus dangereux, c'est ceux qui viennent boire le cappucino en levant le petit doigt et en arrondissant la bouche comme un cul de poule.[8]

This is my role as a Canadian writer of Italian origin living in a mainly French-speaking province. The gap between theory and practice must be crossed — it must become as natural for me to express and interpret the social, political and cultural reality of my adopted land with the same legitimacy as for any other artist or citizen.

From the cultural point of view, Canadian society has reached a crossroads. It must put aside the old reductive concept by which its official spokespersons are either French- or English-speaking. It is time to challenge the idea that a Canadian with an Italian, Slavic, Spanish, Indian or other name is somehow not capable of interpreting the reality to which he or she belongs. The only minority group that has succeeded in doing this up to a certain point has been the Jews. Names like Irving Layton, Leonard Cohen and Mordechai Richler have become points of reference in Canadian literature, yet they are more exceptions that affirm the rule. As Miron writes:

> *Camarade tu passes invisible dans la foule*
> *ton visage disparaît dans la marée brumeuse*
> *de ce peuple au regard épaillé sur ce qu'il voit*
> *la tristesse a partout de beaux yeux de hublot*
>
> *tu écoutes les plaintes de graffiti sur les murs*
> *tu touches les pierres de l'innombrable solitude*
> *tu entends battre dans l'ondulation des épaules*
> *ce cœur lourd par la rumeur de la ville en fuite.*[9]

Cultural minorities still belong to the "voiceless people," as Marco Micone puts it.[10] Yet in the community of Italian-Canadians, we have witnessed an outpouring of talent over the last five or six years. The arrival on the scene of a new generation of intellectuals was marked by the publication of *Roman Candles*, an anthology edited by Pier Giorgio Di Cicco in Toronto in 1978,[11] and by a recent French-language anthology called *Quêtes,* put together by Antonio D'Alfonso and Fulvio Caccia.[12] In Quebec, despite the inevitable tired calls to patriotism and the attempt to exploit an anachronistic form of nationalism, I believe that the presence of minorities will continue to grow and expand. I would go as far as saying that an important part of new culture in our decade will be supplied by third cultures — Italians, French-speaking Jews, Haitians, Greeks, and soon Portuguese, Armenians, Lebanese, etc. From this will spring a new concept of *appartenance* to French Canada.

II
Escaping the Third Solitude

If the 1950s was the era of the two solitudes in Canada, then the 1980s should be seen as the time of the three solitudes. Culturally speaking, French and English Canada remain distant, yet they can still be heard by one another. This is not the case for other minority groups for, in practice, virtually no importance is given to what they have to say about themselves and the rest of the country. There is a tendency to relegate these groups to a no man's land called *multiculturalism* on the federal level and *cultural communities* in the provincial jurisdiction.

In his collection of Italian poetry, Giovanni Di Lullo writes:

> *O figli di nessuno*
> *che correte verso il sole*
> *liberi d'ogni rimpianto,*
> *nell'ora della morte*
> *lasciateci il vostro coraggio.*[13]

The time has come to reevaluate the cultural role of minority groups; 40% of the Canadian population must no longer be ghettoized by what is essentially a paternalist concept. Instead, the officially bilingual — but culturally multicultural — nature of this country must come to the fore. In this decade, multiculturalism must become the shared meeting point of the different components of the Canadian mosaic. This openness to equal polycultural development is a necessity, especially in French Canada, which has historically been locked within its own walls, centred around its racial homogeneity and cultural specificity. True, over the last several years, there has been talk in Quebec about cultural convergence; the government has even been made to adopt the position that "there's more than one way to be Quebecois." But despite this apparent openness, the current government's goal continues to be a brand of Francophone sovereignty, wherein ethnic differences will be gradually absorbed into the *homo quebecencis*. Government authority in Quebec is working toward the acculturation and homogenization of its society, yet this task is doomed to failure, for the new tendency, now that the melting pot theory in the United States has been cast away, is to safeguard and develop cultural roots.

In *Gens du silence* (published in English as *Voiceless People*) by Marco Micone, Nancy expresses this point of view:

> Gino, I teach teenagers who all have Italian names and who have one culture, that of silence. Silence about the peasant origin of their parents. Silence about the manipulation they're victims of. Silence about the country they live in. Silence about the reasons for their silence. Two-thirds of them have hardly finished high school and end up with their parents in the same factories. Those youngsters never come to our meetings or our activities. We have to get to them in the classroom.[14]

In English Canada as in French Quebec, the time

has come for the ethnics of the third solitude to demand the right to speak out and express their different way of living and analyzing their country. And in fact, people of Italian origin, at least in the cultural domain, have been engaged in a quest for identity over the last five or six years. The generations of silence who worked hard to adapt to life in Canada, for financial success and the education of their children, watch with emotion as their exile, their sacrifice, their heroic determination and their need to forge new roots are finally being expressed. Whether the writing is in English, French or Italian, these writers of Italian origin feel the need to speak of their mothers and fathers in their works. This is our generation's confession of love and affection for our parents, and a way of remaining faithful to our roots.

III
The Cultural Specificity and Political Role of Italian Writers in Quebec

In his book *Les Premiers Italiens de Montréal*, Bruno Ramirez writes:

> Mais avant que l'arrivée massive de travailleurs italiens ne jette les bases de ce qui deviendrai la «petite Italie» de Mont-réal, il y a déjà une présence italienne dans la ville. Vers la fin des années 1860, en effet, une cinquantaine de familles d'ori-gine italienne constituent le noyau d'une population qui semble avoir fait du Québec son milieu de vie et de travail. Pour certaines d'entre elles, il ne reste d'italien que le nom; des familles comme les Donegani, les Del Vecchio, les Rus-coni et les Bruchési sont là depuis la fin du XVIIIe et le début du XIXe siècle. [15]

Though the Quebec Italian community has existed for almost a century, its specificity has not had a literary vehicle until very recently. The transition had to be made from a generation of voiceless people struggling to earn their bread to a new group with the luxury of reflection about their own identity, educated enough to be able to "objectivize" themselves and express their particular identity. Socio-political contingencies in Quebec during the Quiet Revolution also stalled the voiceless people's acquisition of a voice. The cultural nationalism of the time worked against the development of cultural difference, since Quebec society in general was in the process of redefining itself. During the 1960s, during this redefinition, heterogeneous voices were not heard; the mentality necessary for maintaining cultural differences did not exist. For social and historical reasons, the Italian community was not able to put its identity on the public agenda for two or three generations. In fact, the Quebecois leading the agonized life had to become a companion of the Americas; the technocrats of Jean Lesage, Robert Bourassa and especially of René Lévesque had to first affirm their French identity before heterogeneous voices like that of the Italian community could emerge.

My generation has claimed its right to be heard, and now we must examine the identity of our voice. The poet Fulvio Caccia is one of those exploring Italian identity in Canada:

La route

Le vent, la route, la traversée
les siècles. Poussières
Où suis-je?
La lumière tombe à plat
sur le bureau verni
Je suis au bord d'un monde
que je ne reconnais pas

La musique tresse
des nattes au silence

La cuisine éructe
énormément
Seize heures
l'heure ténue déclinante
Le jour est une planète secrète
pivotant au centre de ma chambre
petit vortex quotidien.[16]

I myself have had to reflect upon my identity: I have had to grasp my own dimension in relation to those Quebec poets and writers whose families have been here for generations. I have felt spiritual closeness and affection reading Quebec poets, especially Gaston Miron, because their self-affirmation is similar to my search in some ways. I like to hear the Quebec artist declare out loud his irreversible appartenance to his geographical milieu; he is stating his right to a specific identity without external constraints; in a certain way during the same years I felt a similar need for belonging. But on the other hand I realize that the historical vision of Quebec that the intelligentsia and the Péquistes offer does not correspond to what I feel; the defeat on the Plains of Abraham and that of the Patriotes in 1837 did not leave indelible psychic scars on me. Psychologically, I am not part of a colonized people, and besides, my sensitivity is fundamentally Mediterranean and Southern even if I have been transplanted to Northern climes. My sensitivity was and remains centred around a conflictual imagery between warmth and cold, between the peasant and the industrialized world, between the awareness of belonging to an illustrious and plurisecular cultural tradition and the will to define myself in relation to a culture *in fieri*, still in search of its own specificity and value. My deepest concern has been to send roots down into Quebec soil, while referring back to the Italian presence in Canada since the time of the great explorers of the European colonization. And so my desire to incorporate the historical dimension in my writing.[17]

Of course, defining the present and future of Italian Quebec writing is no easy task, for this new literature is in full development. Yet I am convinced that, historically, the appearance of a new set of themes in French writing in Canada can only enrich it. Authors of Italian origin feel the need to express their own perceptions of Quebec reality, just as Quebecois writers have done over the past two decades. One of the fundamental goals that I and other Italian Quebec writers have is the recovery and interpretation of our history. We must develop the will and the ability to retrace our historical roots and interpret Canadian and Quebec reality from our experience and sensitivity, as Italian-Americans have already done. Francis Ford Coppola's film *The Godfather* represents an important step in creating Italian roots in the United States. Beyond the mafioso ritual and mythology, especially in the second part, this film includes an attempt to see American history through an Italian perspective. This is the sort of cultural undertaking that interests me in the Canadian and Quebec context, and I would like to see Italian-Canadian authors expressing Canada and Quebec as Italians. Unfortunately, whether in academic research or literary creation, until a few years ago we were simply subjects of interpretation.

Yet now, for the first time, among both English- and French-speaking Italian-Canadians, there is a generation of intellectuals capable of interpreting themselves and the rest of the country. This remarkable leap forward will grow and expand in the years to come and shake preconceived notions and old analytical limits. No doubt this dialectic will disturb some, but it will create a new set of themes which in the long run, I'm sure, will enrich Canadian and Quebec society as a

whole. I will conclude with these verses from Gilles
Vigneault:

De mon grand pays solitaire
Je crie avant que de me taire
A tous les hommes de la terre
Ma maison c'est votre maison
Entre mes quatre murs de glace
Je mets mon temps et mon espace
A préparer le feu la place
Pour les humains de l'horizon
Et les humains sont de ma race. [18]

NOTES

1 Gilles Vigneault, "La Chanson du temps perdu," *Avec les vieux mots* (Quebec City: Editions de l'Arc, 1964, p. 67).

2 Gaston Miron, "Fragment de la vallée," *Courtepointes* (Ottawa: Editions de l'Université d'Ottawa, 1975, p. 19). Cf. *L'Homme rapaillé* (Montréal: Les Presses de l'Université de Montréal, 1970). Published in English as *Embers and Earth*, D.G. Jones and Marc Plourde, translators (Montreal: Guernica Editions, 1984).

3 Gaston Miron, "Demain, l'histoire," *op. cit.*, p. 33.

4 Gratien Gélinas, *Hier les enfants dansaient* (Ottawa: Les Editions Leméac, 1968, p. 32).

5 Gilles Vigneault, "Mon pays," *op. cit.*, p. 15.

6 Philippe Haeck, "Caresses morsures tout ensemble," *La Nouvelle barre du jour*, No. 100-101. March 1981, p. 96.

7 Claude Beausoleil, "Lectures d'errances actuelles," *La Nouvelle barre du jour*, No. 129, September 1983, p. 89.

8 Marco Micone, *Addolorata* (Montreal: Guernica, 1984, p. 61).

9 Gaston Miron, "Le Camarade," *op. cit.*, p. 27.

10 Marco Micone, *Voiceless People*, translated from French by Maurizia Binda (Montreal: Guernica, 1984). Published in French as *Gens du silence* (Montreal: Québec/Amérique, 1982).

11 Pier Giorgio Di Cicco, editor, *Roman Candles: An Anthology of Poems by Seventeen Italo-Canadian Poets* (Toronto: Houndslow Press, 1978).

12 Antonio D'Alfonso and Fulvio Caccia, editors, *Quêtes: Textes d'auteurs italo-québécois* (Montreal: Guernica, 1983).

13 Giovanni Di Lullo, *Il fuoco della pira* (Montreal: Edizioni Simposium, 1976, p. 76).

14 Marco Micone, *op. cit.*, p. 71.

15 Bruno Ramirez, *Les Premiers Italiens de Montréal* (Montreal: Le Boréal Express, 1984, p. 12).

16 Fulvio Caccia, *Irpinia* (Montreal: Guernica/Triptique, 1983, p. 34).

17 Filippo Salvatore, *Suns of Darkness* (Montreal: Guernica, 1980). Also *La Fresque de Mussolini* (Montreal: Guernica, 1985).

18 Gilles Vigneault, 'Mon pays," *op. cit.*, p. 14.

ANTONIO D'ALFONSO

The Road Between: Essentialism. For an Italian Culture in Quebec and Canada

I

In 1977 I was living and working in Ottawa for a multi-national, spending my days trying to figure out a way to frame the written word on the computer "page." It was my first real job outside the universities. It was also my first real contact with the bureaucratic world. It was not so much the job that kept me there as much as the money it brought me and, especially, the free time it left me in the evening. That is when I began to get acquainted with English Canadian literature.

I have a remarkable memory when it comes to remembering events that will have a determining effect on my life. I recall quite well, for instance, the day I walked into an Ottawa bookstore at some busy intersection and fell on a book by a writer about whom I knew little.

I had seen his name already on the list of contributors at the back of literary magazines, but I had till then never gone out of my way to buy one of his books. It was time to do so. I paid a few dollars for *A Burning Patience*. I stepped into a bar, ordered a beer, and began reading the first page I opened. It was page 25 and the poem, "Man without a Country."

Italia bella, I return to you.
There is no question of lateness
for I was taken from you and cannot
remember the parting; there was a sleep and I woke
to the rumours of you...

> *I have traced your features over*
> *my needs over a continent where*
> *I found you out by what I could not love;*
> *patched myself up with*
> *what I hardly knew of you, Italia,*
> *to make a difference stick like dignity,*
> *and now I return, not lately*
> *but finally, maybe to find the patchwork*
> *wrong, or crumble in new possibility*
> *and make myself out as if nothing has happened*
> > *but twenty years.*

Here I was reading whatever it is that makes up CanLit and the first poem I fell onto was about Italy! I closed the book and looked at the author's name. Pier Giorgio Di Cicco. I read the name twice and a third time, and then it dawned on me that the poet was Italian. I re-read the poem about Di Cicco's return to his native land. The word native should be between quotes, since the poem ends by telling us that the poet has no native land, that he has in fact no country at all.

What had this poet to do with Canadian literature? And in which part of my library could I place this particular book? Under what section: CanLit or Italian literature?

1977 was an important year for me. It was the year I became an Italian. One is not born an Italian; one becomes an Italian. Especially when you come from the *campagna*, the country; especially when you are not born in Italy.

1977 was the year I learned that Mary Melfi, Mary di Michele, Pier Giorgio Di Cicco and Marco Fraticelli were Italian names, not English names. Before that I did not know, at least I did not know this as a fact, or if I knew, it was something I refused to admit to my friends or even myself. Being Italian was a fact I was quite unconscious of, or pretended to be unconscious of. Bringing that consciousness to the fore was no easy task. It was like being fished out of the water. Like a fish, as soon as I bit into the bait and was pulled out, I discovered that water was my medium, that *Italianité*, as Paul Valéry put it, was my reality. (Valéry was the son of an Italian mother.)

But what does the knowledge of being an Italian mean? To be a Wop, a worker without a permit, a poet without a language of his own, without a tradition to work in, or to fight against? What does being Italian mean?

Being an Italian is nothing to be frightened of or arrogant about. It is a fact of life, and one must live with it, like one's gender. Of course, you can change your name or the colour of your hair, but at night when you remove all that make-up and look at yourself in the mirror, you will not be able to turn your head away. In many ways, coming to terms with one's *Italianity* is very much like coming out of the closet. Nevertheless you cannot shed overnight the layers of skin you have wrapped yourself in. And you might not even be able to manage it by yourself. The transformation is slow and often painful. You have to *become* yourself. And this is what interests me most: the process of becoming. Struggle is the force behind the process of identity which manifests itself in different ways. Not all struggle, however, need be expressed in stammers or with violence. There exist methods of fighting which require no shouting. They may be invisible to many but remain quite present in those who know what constitutes a struggle.

The process of becoming, the need for struggle: What have these concepts to do with literature? I will try to explain the relationship in terms of Italian-Canadian and Italian-Quebecois writing. First, we will briefly look

at the poetry of Filippo Salvatore and then we will examine other writers.

II

Mi commuovo da sciocco sentimentale
se sente che avete ricevuto una lettera da lontano
e dice che la nonna è ancora malata
e già stanno mietendo il grano,
se sento che t'è nato un bel bimbo maschio
e vedo la tua pupilla di giovane padre brillare,
se sento che l'ami per la prima volta tanto
tanto, è un bel giovane e gli piace lavorare.

Filippo Salvatore
Suns of Darkness

One of the most important encounters in my intellectual
life was Filippo Salvatore. He was the first to explain to
me the particular kind of contribution Italians could
make in Canadian history. When I read his first book,
Tufo e gramigna (1977), I knew from the start that his
participation in the literary world would be recognized.
Besides describing a young man's immigrant experience,
Filippo Salvatore's *Tufo e gramigna* analyses man's
never-ending search for balance between the natural and
the cultural, the Old and New World, between the past
and present, between Italy and Canada, between the
country and city, between art and non-art. With his
book Filippo Salvatore was the first of the few writers
working in Italian to question the physical matter of
poetry.

*

Salvatore's poetry takes its form in two ways. The

first is a versification which "imitates" everyday *speech*: the style follows speech mannerisms whereby the poet writes as a common person. The second is a more complex, more hermetic sort of verse-making. It is a writing influenced by a literary tradition going as far back as the origins of poetry; it is the *literary* style whereby the common person speaks as a poet. This conscious movement from one form of writing to another — from the *spoken* to the *written* word and from the *written* to the *spoken* word — demonstrates quite clearly how departure from and the return to origins is tightly knitted in the material structure of Salvatore's poetry.

Tufo e gramigna (translated and published in 1980 as *Suns of Darkness*) is not the diary of a young poet. It is, on the level of form we were speaking about, the fundamental search of one person wishing to fix himself in the role of the poet without however wanting to lose his personal essence in the process. The *person* wants to control the poet and not to become his slave. Because one is not better than the other Salvatore must continually move from one position to another, and it is this movement of form which unconsciously prepares the reader to accept the tragedy described by the poet. The poet begins with the use of everyday speech (the spoken word), the natural, and gradually heads for the written word (the literary word), the cultural. This transformation eventually provokes a peculiar type of *formal tragedy* which will attain its climax the moment the poet realizes the need to "go back," to "return" to the spoken word, to the person, and yet is unable to succeed unless he uses the only feasible form: the written word.

And so, paradoxically, it is by becoming more and more cultural, by writing a determined kind of poetry, basing himself on the tacit rules imposed by traditional rhyme schemes and meter — such as can be found in the *sestina* "Eldorado" (not published in *Suns of Darkness*) — that the poet finally meets the *person*. The poet must therefore become not only a poet, but an *erudite* poet. This learned poet cannot, however content himself with what he finds in books; he has to learn to use his tools in a way not foreseen by the literary norms of the past. He begins to blaspheme, if we can call it that. No longer is the sestina the love poem Arnaut Daniel, Petrarca or Dante meant it to be; the sestina becomes a *loving* poem about the natural life the poet has lost.

There is only one exit from this apparent *impasse*: it is the synthesis of the natural-cultural confrontation, having the natural foisted on the cultural world. This dialectic produces a movement and from this movement comes the outcry of revolt. The poet screams and puts into question culture. But he does not want to be alone in his revolt. He sides with other poets who, like him, fight against the Insensitive Machine. The last poems of *Tufo e gramigna*, reprinted and translated in *Suns of Darkness*, entitled *Sirventi*, are dedicated to those "friends" — Pablo Neruda, Gaston Miron, Pier Paolo Pasolini, Alekos Panagoulis and the Basques — who, like Salvatore, believe in a possible union of the natural and cultural worlds, a union of *dignity*. This is the spiritual departure from tragedy, a struggle which kindles the lasting source of hope: the hope of finding the respect for life and human dignity:

Fratelli, riflettete
sul senso della vita,
possiamo amarci ancora.

It is obvious, Filippo Salvatore arrives at this balance through great emotional stress, an agony present everywhere in his work; he therefore naturally identifies with the other agonized poet, Gaston Miron.

214

The search for a country is not a question of nationalism. It is a more subjective kind of quest: Miron called it "national consciousness." Salvatore's poet cannot be satisfied by any one type of nationalism. Take, for example, the conversation between the poet and his grandfather living in Italy, described in "E' pura verità":

Non è meglio mangiare lontano
che restare qui a patire la fame?
(...) Amala quella terra d'oltre mare,
non è il paradiso, anch'io la conosco,
ma t'ha dato l'essenziale...
E che si campa a fare se non si vuol lottare?
Saluta il sangue nostro
sparso per il mondo; scriveteci spesso,
non ci dimenticate; bastano solo alcuni righi
per dirci come state.

The grandfather insists on telling his grandson, who has intentions of returning to live in Italy to go back to Quebec for it "may not be Paradise, but it has given you the essentials." This however does not calm the poet's need to find a land where he may live happily. Where can happiness be found? Happiness will not come from a country, at least that is what is implied in the conversation between the grandfather and grandson. Happiness can only come from something more abstract, a living space. One must struggle for this space as the grandfather says, *"E che si campa a fare se non si vuol lottare?"*

What the poet desires is a space large enough to cover the hiatus between two worlds, a space which can serve as an intersection for different realities. Salvatore never boasts about the beauties of one land to the detriment of the other; both worlds possess their qualities and faults. The poet only wishes to reconcile that which is unreconcilable in his reality; the poet's role is to synthesize that which would naturally collide.

Nature alone cannot be the solution; nature can be good only if it is invested with elements of the cultural world. What is desirable in fact is not nature in its pure form but a nature to the power of two, nature that has been transformed by an external force, nature that has moved one notch higher.

After the blind identification with nature and the no less blind projection onto the cultural world, the poet must now discover an unnamed territory: an amalgamation of innocence and culture, a style which we could call *essentialism*. By this definition an *essential* poet is one who not only finds a point of intersection, no matter how durable or ephemeral, for all the contradictory forces working within and without him, but also a new language or a new way of using the language he chooses. A poet who finds himself in such a *situation* cannot be expected to vacuously adhere to the norms prescribed by the tradition imposed by the language he chooses. If anything, the essential poet is obliged to re-invent a way of expressing himself. How can such a poet ever be a traditionalist? He would be naturally inclined to become a modernist rather than a traditionalist.

III

Art has always been deeply rooted in a country's social context. Even the artists who in the past created work outside their contemporary situation did so in a socially conscious manner. So, the modern artist. Art involves a sense of duty. A person rarely creates in solitude. He must act, whether he likes it or not, through the need to do that which must be done at a particular moment, in a particular context.

During the Seventies, art in general and poetry in particular were heading towards a major change in Canada and Quebec. The transformation was obviously not only domestic; it occurred in other countries as well. However it was only once we acknowledged the mutations brought about by the American counter-culture and European existentialism, structuralism, and semiology that Canadian and Quebecois artists decided to adapt themselves to what they had learned from other artists. One glance at the books published in Quebec during the Seventies suffices to make us realize how fundamental this metamorphosis was. Writers such as Philippe Haeck, Claude Beausoleil, André Roy, Nicole Brossard, Yolande Villemaire, Jean Yves Collette, Michel Gay and Roger Des Roches, just to name a few, are very much the products of their times, and are undoubtely among the finest poets ever to come out of Quebec.

Poets acted not as individuals but as groups and this enabled their solitary experimentations to be taken seriously. As a result laboratory studies turned into powerful schools of thought. On the one hand, Quebecois authors put to practice in fiction the literary theories expounded by Roland Barthes, Jacques Derrida, and Philippe Sollers; on the other hand, Canadian writers such as Bill Bissett, George Bowering, B.P. Nichol, Artie Gold, searched for inspiration in the United States, in such writers as Frank O'Hara, Charles Olson, and Gary Snyder.

This polarization had its negative aspects. If you wrote in French and did not belong to the *Modernité* group, or if you wrote in English and did not belong to the regional "in-power" group, you simply did not stand a chance of ever seeing your work in print. You might eventually find an interested publisher willing to pay for the printing of your collection of poems but you would never receive the attention your work deserved. You were left out in the cold for no other reason than for being alone. You had to belong.

*

When a group of writers tyrannically forces fashions upon readers and other writers, fashions which limit the writing style that will be published there are few alternatives: you either adhere to what is in style or you remain a provincial writer. You can choose to adapt to the formal styles pouring in through the borders, or create an illusory world of Canadian traditions. However a third alternative does exist, a synthesis of these two extremes. It retains the freedom of modernism and the discipline of traditionalism. This third thread runs between the other two, crossing them through and through. I call this third alternative *essentialism*.

Despite the different literary styles of Italian writers in Canada and Quebec and their divergent views, we begin to hear an Italian voice coming through their works. As a result of this new voice an Italian tradition is being felt in the writing of this land.

When we speak of an Italian tradition it is well to keep in mind that Italy is a land of many languages. The Italian language we hear on radio or on T.V. Sunday mornings is not the language I was taught to speak as a child; it is not a mother tongue for many of the writers mentioned above. That official language is a foreign language, a dialect spoken mostly in the Tuscany region.

Now in order to understand one another we have to find a neutral ground, a third language. Sometimes this becomes the English language; other times it is French. It is only very recently that we have chosen to speak to one another in Italian, that is, in Italy's official language. (According to the Italian magazine *L'Espresso* in the September 1984 issue, the Italian language until the Seventies was spoken by less then 30% of the population, however in less than ten years this percentage grew, thanks to schooling and children speaking Italian in their homes forcing their parents to assimilate the Italian vocabulary. This is what happens to an Italian child when he goes to a French or English school in this country and speaks these languages with his parents at home.)

We wish to speak a language of communication. We want to get out of the Tower of Babel in which history emprisoned us. It is the first time in the history of Quebec we, as a group of Italian writers and intellectuals, have voluntarily chosen to come closer together and become conscious of our identities. *Difference*, or the awareness of being different, has finally dawned on us.

Whether we write in French or English or Italian our Italian voice begins to be heard, a voice unlike anything we have ever heard in this nation before. To read an Italian writer working in this country is not to read a Quebecois or Canadian writer.

The voices do not follow an identical melody, yet the harmonies do not antagonize each other. Perhaps that is why there are as many visions of being Italian as there are Italian writers in Canada and Quebec. In this aspect we are quite faithful to the Italian tradition: the view of the world we depict is personal, as disparate as our diversified works. Our world resembles a mosaic.

Many of the writers come from peasant backgrounds, their parents were small landowners or *contadini* working for *latifondisti*. It is no wonder then to find in their works preoccupations common to the peasant or the peasant become a city-dweller and bourgeois. The city has obviously left its mark on these images and, more often than not, it is the city that has made it possible for these writers to find their own individual style.

Mary Melfi, Mary di Michele, Marco Micone, Filippo Salvatore come, as I do, from the Abruzzi (Abruzzo and Molise regions). It is natural that our writings bear some resemblances to the kind of hopes we possess, the fears which haunt us. Cities look like Charybdis and Scylla; men and women search for fathers; our outcries sound like Dido's laments; our verve is like Aeneas's verve and our feasts always have a Circe among the guests. The list of similarities is long but one thing is clear: the symbolism is specific — the reverberation of a particular people.

To describe Italian writers in Quebec Fulvio Caccia uses the image of the phoenix which rises in the morning from its ashes — presage of birth after death: the present must end in death for the future to come to life. How this future will come about each one of us is free to speculate. The solution lies in creativity. Is it the fear of dying which kindles the Italian writer to create? We have no choice when he find ourselves face to face with the final silence: we have to scream now. It is thanks to this scream that we were able to recognize one another's voice, that we walked towards one another to talk and compare notes and findings. The literary space is a laboratory where we study the fragments of our past, where a future built to our scale shall be designed.

If Italian writers in Canada and Quebec want to leave their indelible traces on our culture they must study and absorb Italian literary tradition as well as English and French. When I speak of Italian literature I also include modern writers in Italy, those not published in the Oscar Mondadori *Poesia* series or in Einaudi's *Nuovi Coralli* or *Gli Struzzi* series.

To believe that an Italian writer can make it on his own is wishful thinking. One look at any culture, in any country, should suffice to discourage the solitary wanderer. The only way to win public esteem as a writer coming from another literary tradition is by allowing the people of the adopted country to understand the workings of his particular tradition.

Beauty is not inborn, it is the fruit of learning. Beauty has to be taught. Dante Gabriel Rossetti (also from the Abruzzi) spent most of his life translating the Italian poets who had influenced his work and contributed to the making of this century's greatest American poet, Ezra Pound. Thanks to Rossetti's translations the English were able to discover Dante and appreciate early Italian literature.

If Italian writers in this country wish to be taken seriously, they will have to work very seriously at trying to render intelligible their complex traditions not only to other peoples in this land but to themselves. We should not take for granted that people comprehend all the intricacies of our popular myths and lifestyles. Those who have been most successful in teaching the Quebecois and Canadian audiences to fully assimilate the mechanisms of Italian culture are the novelist, Frank Paci, and the playwright, Marco Micone.

Perhaps, their medium has permitted them to refuse death and to adapt themselves to the different tastes of their public. This is why, contrary to Fulvio Caccia, I believe the best image to describe what Italian writers are is not the phoenix, but the chameleon: death is not necessary, only a change of colour suffices to allow adequate access into the new society. And it is the power of adaptation that will permit us to accomplish the enormous task we have set ourselves, consciously or unconsciously: the welding of cultures: the Canadian (English), the Quebecois, the Italian, and for those Italian writers working in Germany, Australia, Argentina, Brazil, and elsewhere, the cultures and languages of their adopted countries.

We have to become iconoclasts, and in our different ways, destroy the stereotypes and false ideas people have of Italians. To see a play by Marco Micone is not only to experience the Italian culture on a stage, but also the criticism of that culture living in an artistic world. What is important about a Micone play is how it is a play on itself. His plays *are* plays and do not pretend to be plays, that is scenes presented on a stage re-enacted by actors who have learned their lines. Micone is a true essential writer. He did not choose drama, drama chose him. *Gens du silence* (*Voiceless People*) and *Addolorata* are stories about Italians, Italians looking at Italians, Italians looking at a Quebecois public, Italians playing at theatre. When the audience applauds at the end of a Micone play it is the artist they cheer.

IV

Objects are not as fragile as the Sixties said they were. We have modified certain things, but fundamentally it is we who have changed most. We who believed we could have the world just by asking for it, realize that the world is not ours to take. It is always the world that takes us when it wants. That is the lesson the Seventies taught us; the harsh fact of a reality we thought we could fashion to our desires.

The Seventies however are not the Eighties. If conformity symbolizes the decade that ended a few years ago, the Eighties represent, if not radical change, then a definite adaptation to a metamorphozed environment.

Being a product of the growling Sixties, I hoped for a more radically involved decade, but it is not quite so, that is, it is not the radical decade I had wished for. Or perhaps it is, and it is I who do not understand what this new radicalism means. The Eighties are probably more radical than I imagine; so radical in fact that the common meaning of the word *radical* does not encompass what we are going through as a people today.

Radical comes from the Latin *radix*, which means root, and is synonymous in the English language with essential. I am sure that there are many people today who would never describe the Eighties as being an essential era or, if you prefer, a decade of essence. Yet when Marco Fraticelli shows me his computer poems, I know the Eighties are precisely that: a decade of the essence, a *going towards* the roots of it all. The computer and other inventions in this technological world are teaching us much about how our minds function. They enable us to take a giant step outside the small dreamworlds we built for ourselves back in the Sixties.

These creations are forcing me to *adapt* myself to the worlds I create, instead of confronting them with half-truths. I am learning to take what I need from these worlds I am part of, take what I need so that I can give myself more fully. It is time I start writing for the young people, for they are my potential readers. It is they who will help me attain old age. This is why it has become imperative we build a solid modern cultural foundation upon which the present and future world can grow.

There can be no large economic or industrial project without a firm cultural foundation. Architects and civil engineers have to read. The same is true of politicians. There can be no politics without a culture. It is the poet who pushes his friends to create a publishing house. And it is a publishing house started by friends of the poet which power the motors of the cultural economy of a country. If writers such as Marco Fraticelli, Filippo Salvatore, Mary Melfi, Ken Castellano-Norris, Fulvio Caccia, and Marco Micone did not exist, I would never have started Guernica Editions, nor would I ever have published my own writings. If writers such as Mary di Michele, Pier Giorgio Di Cicco, Alexandre Amprimoz, and Frank Paci did not exist, a symposium on Italian writing in Canada held in Italy would never have been possible. If there is culture, if there are cultural artefacts, there will be economy and politics.

When *La poesia italiana nel Quebec* came out in 1983, I was impressed. I read all twenty-six writers, from page 1 to page 140. As I closed the book I came to the conclusion that not all the poets included in Caticchio's anthology deserved the title of Sunday writer. Poets like Tonino Caticchio, Giovanni Di Lullo, Luigi Di Vito, Corrado Mastropasqua, Augusto Tomasini, and certainly Fulvio Caccia and Filippo Salvatore, would have no difficulty getting their works published and reviewed in the finest literary magazines.

> Com'era freddo que l'appartamento
> de via Frattina centoventitré:
> 'na cucinetta co' quer paravento
> ch'era salotto e cammera pe' me.
> Pe' quanti mesi me ce nasconnesti
> que l'inverno freddo der quarantatré?
> "Finchè saremo libberi, dicesti,
> 'sto nasconnijo qui appartienne a te!"
> Poi que la sera... zitto! hanno bussato!
> Scappai dar tetto... dissi solo addio...
> Fosti arestata p'avé rifuggiato
> un certo Moscadé ch'era giudio.
> Stetti nascosto a Terni da Nannina
> poi venne l'alleato americano:
> rientrai a Roma... giunsi a Via Frattina...
> bussai... me tremavano le mano!
> "L'hanno ammazzata qui, proprio qui drento,
> disse er portiere... e pe' sarvatte a te!"
> Come'era freddo que l'appartamento
> de Via Frattina centoventitré!

Tonino Caticchio
"Via Frattina, 123"

These poems exhibit a mastery of imagery and carry with them the burden of a literary tradition which we can identify. Caticchio wrote wonderful poems in the Roman dialect. Mastropasqua's Neapolitan poems are songs that bring you straight to the heart of Southern Italy which few writers in Canada or Quebec can capture. With both these "Sunday writers", poetry resides in the *form*, and it is exactly their form which cannot, unfortunately, be translated.

> *'Stu core mio che spasima,*
> *'sta vocca mia c'abbrucia,*
> *solo 'nu nomme teneno:*
> *Femmena.*
> *Tu me turmiente 'a vita,*
> *tu me cunsume 'e ccarne,*
> *tu sulo me cunsuole,*
> *sulo tu.*
> *Femmena, tu pe mme si' comme 'o ffuoco,*
> *m'abbruce si te sto troppo vicino*
> *e sento friddo si te sto luntano.*

Corrado Mastropasqua
"Femmena"

In 1978 when I bought my copy of *Roman Candles*, edited by Pier Giorgio Di Cicco, I had a shock of recognition. It was the first book about being Italian in Canada which united a group of writers. Di Cicco tried to explain how Italian writers, confronted with two cultures, devised a new mode of expressing themselves. Out of the seventeen writers in this anthology, there was a good number whose works had already appeared in the literary magazines of English Canada. Except for a handful of writers not included in this book, *Roman Candles* is an honest collection of poetry whose purpose was the demonstration of hybrid creativity — or, as Di

Cicco called it, *bicultural sensitivity*. *Roman Candles* describes the difficult process of emigrating, of leaving point A and arriving at point B; the difficult realization that B is not better than A, yet pretending that it is. The need to struggle and become is everywhere lacking in a poetry of emigration, for it is too dangerously obsessed with nostalgia. The transcultural solution is a quick but unrealistic way out of the identity/loss-of-identity crisis. To be able to *go beyond culture* you need to have a culture, a centre of activity, an identity which can be transcended. An Italian in Canada and Quebec cannot be transcultural or a "citizen of the world" unless he is first an Italian. Few writers have actually written about *being* Italian. It is no surprise that the first Italian artists of Quebec were painters; practising the *voiceless* art. It took many years to find our voice, to free ourselves of our oppressive silence. Like a child without a mother-tongue, the Italian writer is a writer without words. He must first learn the meaning of identity and then find the words to express this identity.

For an Italian child to know the meaning of *mother* he must first learn the meaning of *mamma*. How do we Italian writers expect to know who we are if we speak of ourselves in another language? I do not know how this is possible. It is by being ourselves to the core that we will learn to offer the best of ourselves to others, to go beyond ourselves. Universality begins, we know very well, in our home.

Italian-Canadian Voices edited by Caroline Morgan Di Giovanni takes the Italian-in-Canada issue a step further. Suddenly Italians discover they possess a voice. They learned to speak and this anthology offers the Canadian reader a sample of their different *voices*. Italy is not a unity but a mosaic. Italians are seen not as a group but as individuals with distinct identities. This is a very definite step forward. No longer just an abstraction — for what is an Italian?

A look at the Table of Contents of that anthology suffices to prove my point: *First Voices; Roman Candles: The First Anthology; A Mosaic: Selected Short Stories; Identities: Excerpts from the Novels; Presence: Poetry (1979-1983);* and a Bibliography. *Italian-Canadian Voices* is the most important anthology to be published in English about the Italian culture outside Italy. It is a work even the Italians in Italy are learning from. Culture is not geographical but anthropographical. It is no longer the earth but the people that determine a nation. Not just a testimony but a *presence* of a people: such is the subliminal message of *Italian-Canadian Voices*. Not a whisper, but speech. Not only a logos but a lexis. A becoming, a struggle, an identity that is far from being monophonic. A real people with their dignity and suffering and joys. A desire.

> *Silence. Une clarté neuve irise le corail*
> *Lentement, je reviens à moi.*

> Fulvio Caccia
> *Irpinia*

When Fulvio Caccia and I set out to publish our own anthology of Italian writers working in Quebec, we voluntarily widened our scope; we wanted more than the three volumes which preceded *Quêtes*. Our aim was to remain faithful to the Quebec, Canadian and Italian literary traditions. We purposely asked for all types of manuscripts; wishing to go beyond the arbitrary limits imposed by poetry. We called for film scripts, short stories, and chapters from novels. Our first goal was simply to show how Italian writers in Quebec are the products of not two but three different cultures. Without going into an in-depth analysis of the book, I feel that our goal was attained.

My main objection to *Quêtes* is its preface. It is

much too sociological and not literary enough. Somehow I feel it misleads the reader. Instead of introducing the Italian imaginary universe — the social unconsciousness — created — unavoidably expressed — by the eighteen writers included in the anthology, the preface uses all eighteen writers to make a sociological statement.

This leads me to the final point. After more than ten years of trying to come to grips with what I am as a person and, more recently, as a writer and editor, it has become for me quite impossible to take a position on any issue affecting the role of the Italian artist working in Canada and in Quebec.

Some too quickly jump on their horses and wave their Canadian flag; others speak more cautiously and put vague nuances in their affirmations. Others talk of being Quebecois; and another group maintains we remain Italian 100 percent. I am for all four attitudes, unable to content myself with one solution alone.

I have lately put much emphasis on the fact that I remain Italian. It is not necessary that we write in the Italian language. If we do not however, we will have to face our failure to communicate with Italian people in Italy, Germany, Argentina, Brazil, Australia, and other countries where French and English are not spoken. I think we have much to gain in learning to fit ourselves into the Italian tradition. First, because that is where we all fit, being only a generation away from that tradition: up till 1950 our history was the Italian history. Second, because I believe it is necessary to rejuvenate the Italian tradition, rejuvenate it but also expand it to encompass what *Italianità* has become outside Italy. *We may need the Italian tradition as much as the tradition needs us.*

Some of you will rapidly brush with the back of your hand much of what I have just said, claiming that "Canada is my native land", that *"Québec, c'est mon pays"*... I will not disagree with you, I only ask you to look at the Italian experience in its historical perspective, as Marco Micone warns us with the powerful sentence that begins his play, *Gens du silence* (*Voiceless People*):

> *Si l'émigration avait pu aider*
> *à l'émancipation de la classe*
> *ouvrière, elle n'aurait jamais*
> *existé.*
> (If emigration could have helped
> the working class to emancipate
> itself, it would have never existed.)

I do not believe we find ourselves here without a reason. What this reason is, is not easy to say. What we as writers should try to elucidate is how this reason has affected our art. Not only *say* it, but *show* it through our different forms. I know some of you believe we are assimilated, that the acculturation process has begun and cannot be stopped. I do not believe in assimilation, even less in acculturation. I am in favour of difference, both cultural difference and individual difference. It is the task of the Italian writer in Canada and Quebec to help us find these differences.

Selected Bibliography

This bibliography for Italian-Canadian writing contains four lists of titles: one each for works in Italian, in French, in English as well as a sampling of literary and historical studies. Since several authors have publications in more than one language it is best to refer to the lists for all three languages. For the most part the titles are limited to separately published books, but it is well to remember that many of these writers publish regularly in periodicals in English, French or Italian.

Italian Titles

Aconito, Luciano. "Tedium," e "Il sogno," *Canadian Mosaico*, May, 1976, pp. 20-21.

Albani, Elena. *Canada: mia seconda patria*. Bologna: Edizioni Sirio, 1958, 391 pages, novel. Elena Randaccio

Ardizzi, Maria J. *Made in Italy*. Toronto: Toma Publishing, 1982, 216 pages, novel.

_____. *Il sapore agro della mia terra*. Toronto: Toma Publishing, 1984, 259 pages, novel.

Bartocci, Gianni. *In margine a Gauguin*. Padova: Rebellato editore, 1970, 37 pages, poetry.

_____. *La riabilitazione di Galileo: Racconti*. Firenze: Luciano Landi, 1980, short stories.

Bressan, Ottorino. *Non dateci lenticchie: esperienze, commenti, prospettiva di vita italo-canadese*. Toronto: Gagliano Printing, 1962, 150 pages, essays.

Bressani, Francesco Giuseppe. *Breve Relatione* in *The Jesuit Relations and Allied Documents*. ed. Ruben Gold Thwaites. Cleveland: Burrow Brothers Co., 1899, Vols. 38, 39 and 40.

Carli, Camillo. *Razzola amore mio...* Poggibonsi: A. Lalli editore, 1977, 159 pages, novel.

_____. *La giornata di Fabio*. Poggibonsi: A. Lalli editore, 1984, 205 pages, novel.

Caticchio, Tonino. *La storia de Roma*. Montreal: Er Core de Roma editore, 1981, 60 pages, narrative poems.

_____. *La scoperta der Canada*. Montreal: Edizioni Romana, 1981, 94 pages, narrative poems.

_____. *Rugatino*. Montreal: Er Core de Roma editore, 1982, 167 pages, narrative poems.

_____. ed. *La poesia italiana nel Quebec*. Montreal: Centre de Culture Populaire Italien, 1983, 139 pages, anthology of poems in Italian and French.

Conte, Vittoria Ruma. *Raccolta di poesie*. Toronto: Priv. Print., 1977, 32 pages, poetry.

Corea, Antonio Filippo. *I passi*. Catanzaro: Rubbettino editore, 1981, 116 pages, poetry.

D'Alfonso, Antonio. "Il nuovo barocco," *Vice Versa*, Vol. I, No. 1, 1984.

De Facendis, Dario. "Poesie," *Quaderni Culturali*, I, 3-4, 1981.

Di Lullo, Giovanni. *Il fuoco della pira*. Montreal: Edizioni Simposium, 1976, 83 pages, poetry.

Duliani, Mario. *Città senza donne*. Montreal: Gustavo D'Errico editore, 1946, 321 pages, novel.

Fruchi, Dino. *L'Arno racconta: La guerra, l'amore, la vita*. Poggibonsi: A. Lalli editore, 1979, 186 pages, short stories.

Giambagno, Domenica. *Risveglio e Trionfo: poesie d'amore e storie vere*. Toronto: Priv. Print., 1976, 89 pages, poetry.

Grohovaz, Gianni. *Per ricordar le cose che ricordo.* Toronto: Dufferin Press, 1974, 127 pages, poetry.

_____. *Parole, parole e granelli di sabbia.* Toronto: Priv. Print., 1980.

_____. *E con rispetto parlando e al microfono Gianni Grohovaz.* Toronto: Casa editrice sono me, 1983, 251 pages, essays.

La Riccia, Ermanno. *Racconti di emigranti.* Montreal, 1984.

Mastropasqua, Corrado. *'Na lacrema e 'na risa.* Napoli, 1969, poetry.

Menchini, Camillo. *Giovanni Caboto scopritore del Canada.* Montreal: Edizioni Riviera, 1974, 192 pages, history.

_____. *Giovanni Da Verrazzano e la Nuova Francia.* Montreal: Edizioni Simposium, 1977, 264 pages, history.

_____. *Francesco Giuseppe Bressani primo missionario italiano in Canada.* Montreal: Edizioni Insieme, 1980, 170 pages, history.

Papa, Vito. *Poesie del Carpentiere.* Toronto: Priv. Print. 1976, 37 pages, poetry.

Perticarini, Romano. *Quelli della fionda.* Vancouver: Azzi Publishing, 1981, 203 pages, poems, bilingual edition.

_____. *Il mio quaderno di Novembre.* Vancouver: Scala Publishing, 1983, 165 pages, bilingual edition, poetry.

Pirone, Michele. *'N'uocchie e 'na lacrema.* Montreal: Edizioni Pirone, 1974, 126 pages, short stories.

Pisapia, Roberto. *Tiempo ca nun Torneno.* Toronto: Villa Colombo, 1977, 28 pages, poetry.

Ricci, Giuseppe. *L'Orfano di Padre: Memorie di Giuseppe Ricci.* Toronto: Astra Printing, 1981, 253 pages, autobiography.

Rimanelli, Giose. *Biglietto di Terza.* Milano: Mondadori, 1958, 231 pages, travel story in Canada.

Romeo, Luigi. *Battesimo*. Toronto: Dante Society of Toronto, 1963, 47 pages, poetry.

Salvatore, Filippo. *Tufo e gramigna*. Montreal: Edizioni Simposium, 1977, 96 pages, poetry.

Taccola, Umberto. *Una scatola di sole: raccolta di liriche e disegni di viaggio*. Montreal, 1978, poetry.

Tanzi, Gaetano. *Non rompete i coglioni al colonnello*. Roma: Trevi editore, 1981, 82 pages, novel.

Tassinari, Lamberto. *Durante la partenza*. Montréal: Guernica, 1985.

Torres, Matilde. *La dottoressa di Cappadocia*. Roma: Edizioni delle Urbe, 1982, 135 pages, autobiography.

French Titles

Amprimoz, Alexandre. *Chant solaire suivi de vers ce logocentre*. Sherbrooke: Editions Naaman, 1978, 80 pages, poetry.

_____. *Dix, Onze*. Sudbury: Prise de Parole, 1979, 80 pages, poetry.

_____. *Changement de ton*. St. Boniface: Editions des Plaines, 1981, 60 pages, poetry.

_____. *Conseils aux suicidés*. Paris: Editions Saint-Germain des Prés, 1983, 60 pages, poetry.

_____. *Sur le damier des tombes*. St. Boniface: Editions du Blé, 1983, 76 pages, poetry.

_____. *Dix plus un demi*. St. Boniface: Editions du Blé, 1984, 60 pages, poetry.

Caccia, Fulvio. *Irpinia*. Montreal: Editions Triptyque/Guernica, 1983, 64 pages, poetry.

Caccia, Fulvio et Antonio D'Alfonso, eds. *Quêtes: Textes d'auteurs italo-québécois*. Montreal: Guernica, 1983, 280 pages, anthology of poetry, prose and drama.

Campo, Mario. *Coma laudanum*. Montreal: l'Hexagone, 1979, 66 pages, poetry.

_____. *Insomnies polaroids*. Montreal: APLM, 1980, 56 pages, poetry.

D'Alfonso, Antonio et F. Caccia. *Quêtes: Textes d'auteurs italo-québécois*. Montreal: Guernica, 1983, 280 pages, anthology.

D'Apollonia, François. *Réverbérations*. Montreal: Editions du Préambule, 1983, poetry.

De Pasquale, Dominique. *On n'est pas sorti du bois*. Montreal: Leméac, 1972, 86 pages, drama.

Duliani, Mario. *La Ville sans femmes*. Montreal: Société des éditions Pascale, 1945, 316 pages, novel.

_____. *Deux heures de fou rire*. Montreal: Aux editions Serge (Brousseau), 1944, prose.

_____. *Le Règne d'Adrienne*. Paris: Théâtre Daunou, 1935, drama.

Italiano, Carlo. *Les Traîneaux de mon enfance*. Montreal: Tundra, 1974, bilingual collection of stories.

Mascotto, Jacques. *Le Combat perdu de Lenine*. Montreal: St-Martin, 1979.

Micone, Marco. *Gens du silence*. Montreal: Editions Québec/Amérique, 1982, 140 pages, drama.

_____. *Addolorata*. Montreal: Guernica, 1984, 96 pages, drama.

Salvatore, Filippo. *La Fresque de Mussolini*. Montreal: Guernica, 1985, 87 pages, drama.

Turi, Joseph. *Une culture appellée québécoise*. Montreal: Editions de l'Homme, 1971, prose.

Venne, Rosario. *La Chaîne aux anneaux d'or*. Montreal: Editions Chantecler, 1952, poetry.

Zavaglia, Nicola. "Aveuglante lumière," in *Quêtes: Textes d'auteurs italo-québécois*. eds. F. Caccia et A. D'Alfonso. Montreal: Guernica, 1983.

English Titles

Albanese, Vincenzo. *Dead Loves and Tall Angles*. Montreal: Concordia University, 1976, poetry.

Amabile, George. *Blood Ties*. Victoria: Sono Nis Press, 1972, poetry.

_____. *Ideas of Shelter*. Winnipeg: Turnstone Press, 1981, poetry.

_____. *The Presence of Fire*. Toronto: McClelland and Stewart, 1982, 112 pages, poetry.

Amprimoz, Alexandre. *Re and Other Poems*. New York: Vantage Press, 1972, 88 pages, poetry.

_____. *Selected Poems*. Toronto: Hounslow Press, 1979, 80 pages, poetry.

_____. *In Rome*. Toronto: Three Trees Press, 1980, 50 pages, stories.

_____. *Fragments of Dreams*. Toronto: Three Trees Press, 1982, 48 pages, poetry.

Ardizzi, Maria. *Made in Italy*. Toronto: Toma Publishing, 1982, 217 pages, novel, English trans. by A.M. Castrilli.

Bartocci, Gianni. ed. *On Italy and the Italians*. Guelph: University of Guelph, 1974, prose.

Bertelli, Mariella. *The Shirt of the Happy Man*. Toronto: Kids Can Press, 1977, 32 pages, folktale.

Colalillo, Giuliana. *Marco and Michela*. Toronto: James Lorimer, 1978, stories.

D'Agostino, Rosario. "Wake," & 4 poems in *Roman Candles*. ed. P.G. Di Cicco. Toronto: Hounslow Press, 1978, poetry.

D'Alfonso, Antonio. *Queror*. Montreal: Guernica, 1979, 71 pages, poetry.

_____. *Black Tongue*. Montreal: Guernica, 1983, 77 pages, poetry.

_____. *The Other Shore*. Montreal: Guernica, 1985, prose and poetry.

De Iuliis, Celestino. *Love's Sinning Song and other poems*. Toronto: Canadian Centre for Italian Culture and Education, 1981, 60 pages, poetry.

Di Cicco, Pier Giorgio. *The Circular Dark*. Ottawa: Borealis Press, 1977, 65 pages, poetry.

_____. *Dancing in the House of Cards*. Toronto: Three Trees Press, 1978, 63 pages, poetry.

_____. *The Burning Patience*. Ottawa: Borealis Press, 1978, poetry.

_____. *The Tough Romance*. Toronto: McClelland and Stewart, 1979, 96 pages, poetry.

_____. *Flying Deeper into the Century*. Toronto: McClelland and Stewart, 1982, poetry.

_____. *Women We Never See Again*. Ottawa: Borealis Press, 1984, poetry.

_____. ed. *Roman Candles: An Anthology of Poems by Seventeen Italo-Canadian Poets*. Toronto: Hounslow Press, 1978, 85 pages, poetry.

Di Michele, Mary. *Tree of August*. Toronto: Three Trees Press, 1978, 48 pages, poetry.

_____. *Bread and Chocolate*. Ottawa: Oberon Press, 1980, 44 pages, poetry.

_____. *Mimosa and Other Poems*. Oakville: Mosaic Press, 1981, 46 pages, poetry.

_____. *Necessary Sugar*. Ottawa: Oberon Press, 1983, 64 pages, poetry.

_____. ed. *Anything Is Possible. A Selection of Eleven Women Poets*. Oakville: Mosaic Press, 1984, 186 pages, poetry.

Edwards, Caterina. *The Lion's Mouth*. Edmonton: NeWest Press, 1982, 180 pages, novel.

_____. "The Last Young Man," *Journal of Canadian Fiction*, II, 2 (1973), story.

_____. "Island of the Nightingales," *More Stories from Western Canada*. eds Rudy Wiebe and Aritha van Herk. Toronto: Macmillan of Canada, 1980, story.

Fraticelli, Marco. *Instants*. Montreal: Guernica, 1979, 67 pages, poetry.

_____. *Night Coach*. Montreal: Guernica, 1983, 48 pages, poetry.

Gasparini, Len. *Cutty Sark*. Kingston: Quarry Editions, 1970, poetry.

_____. *If You Love*. Ottawa: Borealis Press, 1975, poetry.

_____. *Breaking and Entering: New and Selected Poems*. Oakville: Mosaic Press, 1980, 96 pages, poetry.

_____. *The Climate of the Heart: Poems and Stories*. Cornwall: Vesta, 1982, 81 pages, poems and stories.

Grohovaz, Gianni. *To Friuli from Canada with Love*. Toronto: Astra Printers, 1983, 190 pages, narrative and historical prose.

Italiano, Carlo. *The Sleighs of Old Montreal*. Montreal: Tundra, 1978, stories and pictures.

Lattoni, Liborio. Three poems in *Canadian Overtones: An Anthology of Canadian poetry written originally in Icelandic, Swedish, Norwegian, Hungarian, Italian, Greek and Ukrainian*. trans and ed. Watson Kirkconnell. Winnipeg: Columbia Press, 1935, poetry.

Madott, Darlene. *Song of Silence*. Ottawa: Borealis Press, 1977, 167 pages, Novel.

_____. "The Namesake," *Canadian Ethnic Studies*, XIV, 1 (1982), story.

Maviglia, Joseph. "Eleven Poems," *Poetry Toronto*, 103-4 (1984), poetry.

Mazza, Antonino. *Eugenio Montale, The Bones of Cut-*

tlefish. Oakville: Mosaic Press, 1983, 78 pages, translations of Montale's poems.

Melfi, Mary. *A Bride in Three Acts*. Montreal: Guernica, 1983, 96 pages, poetry.

―――. *A Queen Is Holding a Mummified Cat*. Montreal: Guernica, 1982, 87 pages, poetry.

―――. *The Dance, the Cage and the Horse*. Montreal: D Press, 1976, 90 pages, poetry.

Micone, Marco. *Voiceless People*. Montreal: Guernica, 1984, 96 pages, English translation of play by Maurizia Binda.

Minni, C.D. *Other Selves*. Montreal: Guernica, 1985, short stories.

―――. "Dollar Fever," in *Two Worlds*. ed. Milly Charon. Montreal: Quadrant Press, 1984, short story.

Norris, Ken. *To Sleep, To Love*. Montreal: Guernica, 1982, poetry.

―――. *Whirlwirds*. Montreal: Guernica, 1983, poetry.

Paci, F.G. *The Italians*. Ottawa: Oberon Press, 1978, Signet, 1980, novel.

――. *Black Madonna*. Ottawa: Oberon Press, 1982, novel, 198 pages.

――. *The Father*. Ottawa: Oberon Press, 1984, novel, 193 pages.

Pignataro, Tony. "The Immigrant," *Canadian Mosaico*, 2, 9 (1975), poem.

―――. "My Father," in *Roman Candles*. ed. P.G. Di Cicco. Toronto: Hounslow Press, 1978, poetry.

Pirone, Michele. "Latchkey Children," *Canadian Fiction Magazine*. 20A (1976), short story.

Pivato, Joseph. "His Mother's Funeral," *Voodoo Poetry*. Toronto, 1968.

―――. Three poems in *Poems to Color*. ed. Irving Layton. Toronto: York University, 1970, poetry.

―――. "Petrified Pinch at Piazza Navona, and three

poems in *Roman Candles*. ed. P.G. Di Cicco. Toronto: Hounslow Press, 1978, poetry.

———. "Return to Halifax," in *Italian Canadian Voices*. ed. C.M. Di Giovanni. Oakville: Mosaic Press, 1984, poetry.

Ranallo, Joseph. Two poems in *Roman Candles*. ed. P.G. Di Cicco. Toronto: Hounslow Press, 1978, poetry.

Rossi, Erno. *White Death — Blizzard of '77*. Port Colborne: 77 Publications, 1978, narrative prose.

Salvatore, Filippo. *Suns of Darkness*. Montreal: Guernica, 1980, 85 pages, poetry.

Verdicchio, Pasquale. *Moving Landscape*. Montreal: Guernica, 1985, poetry.

———. *Antonio Porta: Selected Poems*. Montreal: Guernica, 1985, translations of Porta's poetry.

Zingrone, Frank. *Traces*. Toronto: Paradigm Communications, 1980, 61 pages, poetry.

Zizis, Michael. *Translating the Light*. Toronto: Three Trees Press, 1982, 48 pages, poetry.

Literary and Historical Studies

Boissevain, Jeremy. *The Italians of Montreal: Social Adjustment in a Plural Society*. Ottawa: Information Canada, 1970, social history.

Caccia Fulvio, "Les Poètes italo-montréalais: Sous le signe du Phénix," *Canadian Literature*. 106, 1985, essay.

———. *Sous le signe du Phénix: Interviews avec des créateurs italo-québécois*. Montreal: Guernica, 1985.

Caroli, Betty Boyd, R.F. Harney and L.F. Tomasi, eds. *The Italian Immigrant Woman in North America*. Toronto: Multicultural History Society of Ontario, 1978, 386 pages, essays in social history.

Green, Rose Basile. *The Italian-American Novel: A Document of the Interaction of Two Cultures.* Philadelphia: Fairleigh Dickinson University Press, 1974, 414 pages, literary history.

Harney, Robert F. *Dalla frontiera alle Little Italies: Gli italiani in Canada 1800-1945.* Roma: Bonacci Editore, 1984, 313 pages, history.

_____. "Frozen Wastes: The State of Italian Canadian Studies," in *Perspectives in Italian Immigration and Ethnicity.* ed. S.M. Tomasi. Staten Island: American Italian Historical Association, 1977, essays.

Harney, Robert F. and J.V. Scarpaci. eds. *Little Italies in North America.* Toronto: Multicultural History Society of Ontario, 1981, 207 pages, history.

Mastrangelo, Rocco. *The Italian Canadians.* Toronto: Van Norstrand Reinhold, 1979, 64 pages, history, geography and narrative.

Meadwell, Kenneth. "Langue et parole dans l'œuvre poétique d'Alexandre Amprimoz," *Canadian Literature.* 106, 1985, essay.

Mingarelli, Giosafat. *Gli Italiani di Montreal.* Montreal: Centro Italiano d'Attivita Commerciale-Artistiche, 1957, popular history.

Pautasso, Luigi. "La donna italiana durante il periodo Fascista a Toronto, 1930-1940," in *The Italian Immigrant Woman in North America.* eds. Betty Boyd Caroli et al. Toronto: M.H.S.O., 1978, history.

Perin, Robert. "Conflicts d'identité et d'allégeance. La propagande du consulat italien à Montréal dans les années 1930," *Questions du Culture*, 2 (1980), history.

Pivato, Joseph. "The Arrival of Italian-Canadian Writing," *Canadian Ethnic Studies*, XIV, 1, 1982, literary history.

_____. "Documenting Italian-Canadian Writing: A Bibliography," *Italian Canadiana*. 1, 1 (1985), Toronto, history.

Pozzetta, George. ed. *Pane e Lavoro: The Italian American Working Class*. Toronto: M.H.S.O., 1980, 179 pages, social history.

Principe, Angelo. "The Italo-Canadian Anti-Fascist Press in Toronto, 1922-1940," *NEMLA, Italian Studies*, vol. 4, 1980.

Ramirez, Bruno. *Les Premiers Italiens de Montréal: l'origine de la Petite Italie du Québec*. Montréal: Boréal Express, 1984, 136 pages, social history.

Ramirez, Bruno and M. Del Balso. *The Italians of Montreal: From Sojourning to Settlement, 1900-1921*. Montreal: Editions du Courant, 1980, social history.

Spada, A.V. *The Italians in Canada*. Montreal: Italo-Canadian Ethnic and Historical Research Centre, 1969, 387 pages, social history.

Sturino, Frank. "Family and Kin Cohesion Among Southern Italian Immigrants in Toronto," in *The Italian Immigrant Woman in North America*. eds. Betty Boyd Caroli et al. Toronto: M.H.S.O., 1978, history.

Vangelisti, Guglielmo. *Gli Italiani in Canada*. Montreal: Chiesa Italiana di N.S. Della Difesa, 1956, 263 pages, social history.

Zucchi, John. *The Italian Immigrants of the St. John's Ward, 1975-1915: Patterns of settlement and neighborhood formation*. Toronto: M.H.S.O., 1981, 43 pages, history.

Addenda

Ardizzi, Maria J., *Conversation with My Son/Conversazione col figlio*. Toronto: Toma Publishing, 1985, 101 pages, poetry.

Barolini, Helen. ed. *The Dream Book: An Anthology of Writing by Italian American Women*. New York: Schocken Books, 1985.

Bonnano, Giovanni, "An Analysis of Frank Paci's Novels," in *Canada: The Verbal Creation/la creazione verbale*. ed. Alfredo Rizzardi. Abano Terme: Piovan editore, 1985, pp. 167-182, literary criticism.

Bruti Liberati, Luigi. *Il Canada, l'Italia e il fascismo, 1919-1945*. Roma: Bonacci Editore, 1984, 254 pages, history.

Catalano, Francis. "Scènes," in *Quêtes*. eds. F. Caccia et A. D'Alfonso. Montreal: Guernica, 1983.

Di Giovanni, Caroline M., ed. *Italian-Canadian Voices: An Anthology of Poetry and Prose (1946-1983)*. Oakville: Mosaic Press, 1984, 205 pages.

Harney, Robert F., ed. *Gathering Place: Peoples and Neighbourhoods of Toronto, 1834-1945*. Toronto: Multicultural History Society of Ontario, 1985, 304 pages, history.

Hutcheon, Linda Bortolotti, "Voices of Displacement," *The Canadian Forum* LXV, 750 (June/July, 1985) 33-39.

La Riccia, Ermanno. *Terra mia: Storie di emigrazione*. Padova: Edizioni Messaggero Padova, 1984, 236 pages, short stories.

MacRan, Elena. *The Sound of a Harp*. Philadelphia: Dorrance and Co., 1976, 279 pages, novel. (Elena Randaccio)

_____. *Diario di una emigrante*. Bologna: Tamari editore, 1979, 112 pages, novel.

Perin, Roberto. "Religion, Ethnicity and Identity:

Placing the Immigrant within the Church," in *Religion/Culture: Comparative Canadian Studies*. eds. William Westfall, Louis Rousseau et al. Canadian Issues, VII. Ottawa: Association for Canadian Studies, 1985.

Pivato, Joseph, "The Return Journey in Italian-Canadian Literature," *Canadian Literature*, 106 (Fall, 1985).

Powe, Bruce W. *A Climate Charged: Essays on Canadian Writers*. Oakville: Mosaic Press, 1984, 196 pages, criticism.

Razzolini, Esperanza Maria. *All Our Fathers: The North Italian Colony in Industrial Cape Breton*. Halifax: International Education Centre, St. Mary's University, 1983, 55 pages, history.

Riedel, Walter, ed. *The Old World and the New: Literary Perspectives of German-speaking Canadians*. Toronto: Univ. of Toronto Press, 1984. Literary history and criticism.

Simon, Sherry. "Speaking with Authority: the Theatre of Marco Micone," *Canadian Literature*, 106 (Fall, 1985).

Amprimoz, Alexandre. *Hard Confessions*. Winnipeg: Turnstone Press, 1987.

Ardizzi, Maria J. *La Buona America*. Toronto: Toma Publishing, 1987.

Bagnell, Kenneth. *Canadese: A Portrait of the Italian Canadians*. Toronto: Macmillan, 1989.

Bedon, Elettra. *Ma l'estate verrà ancora*. Brescia: La Scuola, 1985.

Castrucci, Anello. *I miei lontani pascoli*. Montreal: Riviera, 1984.

Carducci, Lisa. *Nouvelles en couleurs*. Montreal: Editions Elcee, 1985.

D'Alfonso, Antonio. *L'autre rivage*. Montréal: VLB, 1987.

_____. *L'Amour panique*. Montreal: Lèvres urbaines, 1988.

Di Cicco, Pier Giorgio. *Virgin Science*. Toronto: McClelland & Stewart, 1986.

Di Michele, Mary. *Immune to Gravity*. Toronto: McClelland & Stewart, 1986.

_____. *Luminous Emergencies*. Toronto: McClelland & Stewart, 1990.

Edwards, Caterina. *Homeground*. Montreal: Guernica, 1990.

Mazza, Antonino. *The Way I Remember It*. Toronto: Trans-Verse Prod. 1988.

Michelutti, Dorina, *Loyalty to the Hunt*. Montreal, Guernica, 1986.

Micone, Marco. *Déjà l'agonie*. Montreal: l'Hexagone, 1988.

Minni, C.D. ed. *Ricordi: Things Remembered*. Montreal: Guernica, 1989.

Perin, Roberto & Franc Sturino. eds. *Arrangiarsi: The Italian Immigration Experience in Canada*. Montreal: Guernica, 1989.

Perticarini, Romano. *Via Diaz*. Montreal: Guernica, 1989.

Welch, Liliane. *Word-House of a Grandchild*. Charlottetown: Ragweed Press, 1987.

Zagolin, Bianca. *Une femme à la fenêtre*. Paris: Editions Robert Laffont, 1988.

Zamaro, Silvano. *Autostrada per la luna*. Montreal: Guernica, 1987.

Notes on Contributors

See the bibliography for the titles of works by the contributors.

Alexandre Amprimoz was born in Rome and educated in Italy, France and Canada. He has taught French and Canadian Literature at the Univ. of Manitoba and is now at Brock University, St. Catharines, Ontario. In addition to poetry and prose in English and French he has published studies on Rimbaud and Germain Nouveau.

Robert Billings was born in Niagara Falls, Ontario and has degrees from the University of Windsor and Queen's. A widely published poet and critic, the late Robert Billings was editor with *Quarry*, *Waves*, *Poetry Toronto* and *Poetry Canada Review*. Toronto representative for the League of Canadian Poets, his books include *The Elizabeth Trinities* (Penumbra) and *A Heart of Names* (Mosaic)

Fulvio Caccia was born in Florence, Italy, and educated at the Université du Québec à Montréal. An active French journalist and poet he has been an editor with *Moebius* and *Vice Versa*.

Antonio D'Alfonso was born in Montreal and educated at Loyola College and Université de Montréal. He is a literary critic and poet and as the founder of Guernica Editions has been instrumental in the publication of countless books.

C. Dino Minni was born in Isernia, Italy, and studied at

the Univ. of British Columbia, Vancouver. In addition to many book reviews, in Canadian periodicals his popular short stories have appeared in magazines, anthologies, textbooks and been broadcast on radio. C.D. Minni died in July 1989.

Frank Paci was born in Pesaro, Italy, and has degrees from Univ. of Toronto and Carleton. After some time teaching and working as an editor Paci now devotes his time to writing novels.

Joseph Pivato was born near Vicenza, Italy, and has studied at York Univ. and the Univ. of Alberta (Comparative Literature). He has taught at Athabasca Univ. in Edmonton and has published in many literary journals such as *Il Caffé*.

Filippo Salvatore was born in Campobasso, Italy, and has degrees from McGill Univ. and Harvard Univ. in Italian. He has taught at Chaplain College, Université de Montréal and is now at Concordia Univ. His English, French and Italian poetry and prose have been published in many countries.

Roberta Sciff-Zamaro was born in Friuli, Italy, and has degrees from Università di Venezia, Ca' Foscari, and Univ. of Alberta (Comparative Literature) where she has taught Italian.

Sante A. Viselli was born in Italy and has a doctorate from Université Paul Valery, Montpellier, France. He has published work on French and Canadian writing, and teaches French at Memorial University in St. John's, Nfld.

Index of Writers

Aconito, L., 233
Addison, J., 56
Albani, E., 172, 183-184, 188, 233
Albanese, V., 238
Allott, M., 60
Amabile, G., 238
Amprimoz, A.L., 13, 30, 68, 101-120, 180, 223, 236, 238
Aquin, H., 22, 163, 167
Ardizzi, M.J., 12, 30, 103, 172, 175-177, 180, 183-188, 233, 238, 245
Atwood, M., 23-24, 33, 49, 60, 67, 70, 90, 99, 105, 187
Aubert de Gaspé, P.-J., 19
August, R., 28-29, 34

Bacon, F., 39
Balzac, H. de, 43
Barthes, R., 217
Bartocci, G., 180, 233, 238
Barolini, H., 245
Bassani, G., 171
Bauer, W., 30
Baudelaire, C., 111, 120
Baudrillard, 165
Beausoleil, C., 196, 206, 217

Beckett, S., 38, 45
Bertelli, M., 238
Bertrand, C., 155, 166
Bessai, D., 33
Bessette, G., 21
Billings, R., 13, 121-152
Bissett, B., 217
Blodgett, E.D., 17-18, 33-34
Blouin, J., 167
Bly, R., 128
Boehme, J., 51
Boissevan, J., 242
Bonnano, G., 245
Borson, R., 125-135, 138-149, 152
Bosco, M., 67
Bossuet, 112
Bowering, G., 217
Bowering, M., 152
Bowra, C.M., 55, 60
Bressan, O., 233
Bressani, F.G., 172, 187, 234
Bringhurst, R., 128
Bronte, E., 43
Brossard, N., 217
Bruti Liberati, L., 245
Bugnet, G., 20
Buckler, E., 41, 46, 56, 60

Byron, G.G., 56

Caboto, G., 107
Caccia, F., 13, 14, 104, 111,
    120, 153-167, 184, 188, 199,
    202, 206, 220, 221, 223, 224,
    227, 236, 237, 242
Callaghan, M., 22, 69
Campo, M., 237
Carli, C., 180, 234
Caroli, B.B., 242
Carman, B., 151
Carrier, R., 22, 75
Catalano, F., 245
Caticchio, A., 5, 14, 158, 166,
    180, 184, 187, 224-225, 234
Cavalcanti, G., 171
Chekhov, A., 69
Clarke, A., 65
Cohen, L., 198
Colalillo, G., 238
Collette, J.Y., 217
Conn, J., 129, 152
Conrad, J., 118
Conte, V.R., 234
Corea, A.F., 172, 179, 187,
    234
Cornelisen, A., 187
Creighton, D.G., 25-26
Croisset, 42
Cross, M., 24-25, 33
Crozier, L., 152

D'Agostino, S., 103-104, 118-
    120, 151, 238
D'Alfonso, A., 14, 104, 111,
    113, 120, 158, 160-161, 166,
    184, 188, 199, 206, 207-229,
    234, 237, 238
Daniel, A., 214
Dante, 111, 113, 115, 171,
    214, 221

Danylchuk, I., 26
D'Apollonia, F., 237
David, C., 184
Davey, F., 33
de Assis, M., 76
Debray, R., 155, 166
De Facendis, D., 234
Defoe, D., 42
de Grandpré, P., 21
Deleuze, G., 155-156, 166, 167
Dempster, B., 127, 129
Derrida, J., 217
De Iuliis, C., 239
De Masi, G., 184
De Pasquale, D., 237
Descartes, R., 39
Des Roches, R., 217
Di Cicco, P.G., 14, 27, 104-
    120, 125-129, 151, 158, 166,
    180-183, 188, 198, 206, 210,
    223, 225, 239
Di Giovanni, C.M., 14, 75,
    158, 166, 226, 245
Di Lalla, M., 184
Di Lullo, G., 166, 172, 179,
    187, 199, 206, 224, 234
Dimić, M.V., 34
Di Michele, M., 11, 104, 113,
    116-117, 120, 121-152, 158,
    166, 180, 210, 220, 223, 239
Di Vito, L., 224
Donnell, D., 129
Dostoevsky, F., 43
Dryden, J., 56
Ducharme, R., 163-164, 167
Dudek, L., 151
Duhamel, R., 21
Duliani, M., 13, 26, 31, 172-
    174, 187, 234, 237

Eckhart, M., 51-52
Eco, U., 151

Edel, L., 129
Edwards, C., 32, 34, 64, 73-75, 184, 186, 188, 239
Eggleston, W., 25, 33

Faulkner, W., 45, 51
Ferron, J., 75
Ferron, M., 76
Flaubert, G., 42-43, 51
Fraticelli, M., 104, 115, 120, 210, 223, 240
Friedman, I., 71
Fruchi, D., 180, 234
Frye, N., 23-25, 27, 34, 128
Fuentes, C., 76

Gallant, M., 69-70
Gasparini, L., 104-120, 151, 240
Gatenby, G., 129
Gay, M., 217
Gelin, L., 21
Gelinas, G., 193, 206
Giambagno, D., 234
Gilbert, S., 97, 99
Glickman, S., 125-135, 138, 141-144, 152
Gold, A., 217
Graves, R., 88-90, 99
Gobard, H., 156, 166
Green, R.B., 243
Greenstein, M., 33
Grohovaz, G., 172, 179, 180, 187, 235, 240
Guattari, F., 155-156, 166
Gubar, S., 97, 99

Haeck, P., 195-196, 206, 217
Handke, P., 38
Harney, R.F., 34, 243, 245
Harrison, D., 34
Haussmann, 42

Hawthorne, N., 42, 60
Hébert, A., 66, 69, 91, 97, 99
Hegel, G.W.F., 40
Heidegger, M., 56
Heintzman, R.R., 34
Hemingway, E., 54-55, 60, 127
Hemon, L., 20
Homel, D., 189
Hood, H., 66
Hodgins, J., 76
Huch, R., 60
Hutcheon, L.B., 245

Italiano, C., 237, 240

Jackel, D., 33
Jasmin, C., 22
Jonas, G., 23
Jones, D.G., 19, 27, 33, 206
Joyce, J., 43-45, 56, 118

Kafka, F., 42, 118, 155-156, 162, 164, 167
Kahlo, F., 141
Kant, E., 43
Keats, J., 51, 56
Kirkconnell, W., 27, 29, 34
Kierkegaard, S., 111
Klinck, C.F., 21
Kogawa, J., 30-31
Korn, R., 20, 30
Kossein, C., 184
Kreisel, H., 49, 67
Kroetsch, R., 22, 63-65, 75, 186
Kroller, E.M., 34

Lalonde, M., 23
La Riccia, E., 180, 235, 245
Lattoni, L., 27, 240
Laurence, M., 22, 46, 52, 66

Lawrence, D.H., 38, 41, 60
Layton, I., 151, 198
Lee, D., 129
Levine, N., 70
Lillard, C., 27, 34
Locke, J., 43
Lorenzini, A., 120
Lower, A.R.M., 25, 33
Lyotard, 165
Lysenko, V., 30

MacEwen, G., 71-72
MacLennan, H., 22
Macpherson, J., 27
MacRan, E., 245
Madott, D., 69, 240
Maltman, K., 127-129, 134
Mandel, E., 33
Manzoni, A., 171
Marlyn, J., 23, 30, 49
Mazza, A., 118, 151
Martin, C., 75
Mascotto, J., 237
Mastrangelo, R., 243
Mastropasqua, C., 180, 224-
    225, 235
Maupassant, G. de, 60, 69
Maviglia, J., 240
Mazza, A., 240
McLuhan, M., 32, 158
McNeill, J.A., 75
Meadwell, K., 243
Melfi, M., 104-110, 120, 160,
    167, 210, 220, 223, 241
Menchini, C., 235
Merwin, W.S., 128-129
Metcalf, J., 66
Meyrink, G., 163, 167
Micone, M., 12, 14, 30, 120,
    156, 160, 166-167, 177, 197,
    198, 200, 220, 221-222, 223,
    229, 237, 241

Mingarelli, G., 243
Minni, C.D., 12, 13, 61-76,
    180-181, 187, 241
Miron, G., 155, 162, 164, 167,
    192, 198, 203, 206, 214-215
Moisan, C., 23-24, 33, 99
Moliere, 159
Moodie, S., 49
Moore, G.E., 40
Moore, B., 23
Moravia, A., 69, 171
Mouré, E., 129, 151
Morin, M., 155, 166
Moritz, A.F., 127-128
Moses, D.D., 129, 152
Moss, J., 24, 33, 187
Munch, E., 141
Munro, A., 66

Nabokov, V., 48, 60, 118
Neruda, P., 214
Neumann, E., 87-88, 99
Nichol, B.P., 217
Nómez, N., 30
Norris, K., 223, 241
Northy, M., 25

Oates, J.C., 125, 151
O'Hara, F., 217
Olson, C., 217
Oppen, G., 128
Ortega y Gasset, J., 48, 60

Paci, F.G., 12, 13, 30, 35-60,
    65, 68, 79 99, 103, 164, 178,
    180-182, 186-188, 221, 224,
    241
Panagoulis, A., 214
Papa, V., 235
Parent, C., 21
Pavese, C., 112, 128, 151
Pasolini, P.P., 165, 214

Pautasso, L., 243
Perin, R., 243, 246
Perticarini, R., 118, 172, 174-176, 179-180, 187, 235
Petrarca, 115, 214
Pignataro, T., 241
Pirone, M., 180, 235, 241
Pisapia, R., 235
Pivato, J., 9-14, 15-34, 105, 118, 120, 131, 151, 152, 169-188, 241, 243, 246
Pound, E., 113, 221
Powe, B.W., 33, 246
Pozzetta, G., 244
Priest, R., 129, 152
Principe, A., 244
Proust, M., 42
Puzo, M., 204
Pynchon, T., 38

Ramirez, B., 167, 201, 206, 244
Ranallo, J., 242
Razzolini, E.M., 246
Renaud, 163
Ricci, G., 235
Richardson, S., 42
Richler, M., 49, 70, 198
Ricou, L., 24, 33, 99
Riedel, W., 246
Rimanelli, G., 235
Robbe-Grillet, A., 38, 44
Roberts, C.G.D., 19-21, 33, 151
Robin, R., 166, 167
Romeo, L., 27, 236
Ross, S., 22
Rossi, E., 242
Rosenblatt, J., 127
Rossetti, D.G., 221
Rousseau, J.-J., 42-43
Roy, A., 217
Roy, G., 20

Saint John of the Cross, 51
Salverson, L., 30
Salvatore, F., 14, 30, 107-108, 113, 117-118, 120, 161-167, 180, 189-206, 212-215, 220, 223, 224, 236, 237, 242
Sciff-Zamaro, R., 13, 77-99
Scheier, L., 129, 152
Scobie, S., 71
Selvon, S., 31
Shakespeare, W., 41, 51, 159, 162
Simon, S., 246
Skvorecky, J., 27, 30
Smart, C., 125-135, 138, 141-143, 152
Snyder, G., 217
Spada, A., 244
Sollers, P., 217
Sorestead, G.A., 75
Souster, R., 151
Steele, R., 56
Stephansson, S., 20, 26
Stratford, P., 17, 33
Stuewe, P. 24, 33
Sturino, F., 244
Such, P., 129
Suknaski, A., 26
Sullivan, R., 152
Sutherland, R., 22-24, 33
Swift, J., 56

Taccola, U., 236
Tanzi, G., 236
Tassinari, L., 236
Tennyson, A.L., 74
Thériault, Y., 75
Togas, G., 21
Tolstoy, L., 41, 47, 51, 60, 69
Tomasini, A., 224
Torres, M., 172, 178, 187, 236
Tournier, M., 163, 167

Toye, W., 105
Tremblay, M., 163
Trudeau, P.E., 191
Turi, J., 237
Turner, F.J., 25-26, 33
Twain, M., 51

Vachon, G.A., 167
Valery, P., 211
Vangelisti, G., 172, 187, 244
Vargas Llosa, M., 76
Venne, R., 237
Verdicchio, P., 242
Vergil, 113, 171
Vigneault, G., 191-192, 194, 205, 206
Viero, A., 184
Villemaire, Y., 217
Viselli, S., 13, 101-120

Wallace, B., 125-137, 140, 152
Watt, I., 42, 60

Watters, R.E., 34
Wayman, T., 126
Weaver, R., 75
Weil, S., 52
Westfall, W., 246
Wiseman, A., 23, 49
Wittgenstein, L., 45, 55
Wolfe, M., 75
Woodcock, G., 99
Woolf, V. 43-44, 60
Wright, J., 128

Yates, J.M., 27, 34

Zavaglia, N., 237
Zeno, 40
Zingrone, F., 242
Zizis, M., 242
Zola, E., 43
Zolf, L., 34
Zucchi, J., 244

256

Acknowledgements

The editor would like to thank the following:

The Multiculturalism Directorate, Department of the Secretary of State, for providing the funds necessary to make the publication of this book possible.

Athabasca University for granting the editor the sabbatical leave in order to complete this project.

Professor Robert F. Harney and the staff of the Multicultural History Society of Ontario for their support and help.

The contributors for their courage in writing about a new area of study.

David Homel and Martine Leprince for translating the two French essays.

Emma Pivato for her help, support and encouragement.

Pier Giorgio Di Cicco and the other writers for their cooperation.

All the writers and their publishers for letting us quote from their literary works.

And Mary Sabucco Pivato.

Printed by
Ateliers Graphiques Marc Veilleux Inc.
Cap-Saint-Ignace Qué.
in August 1991